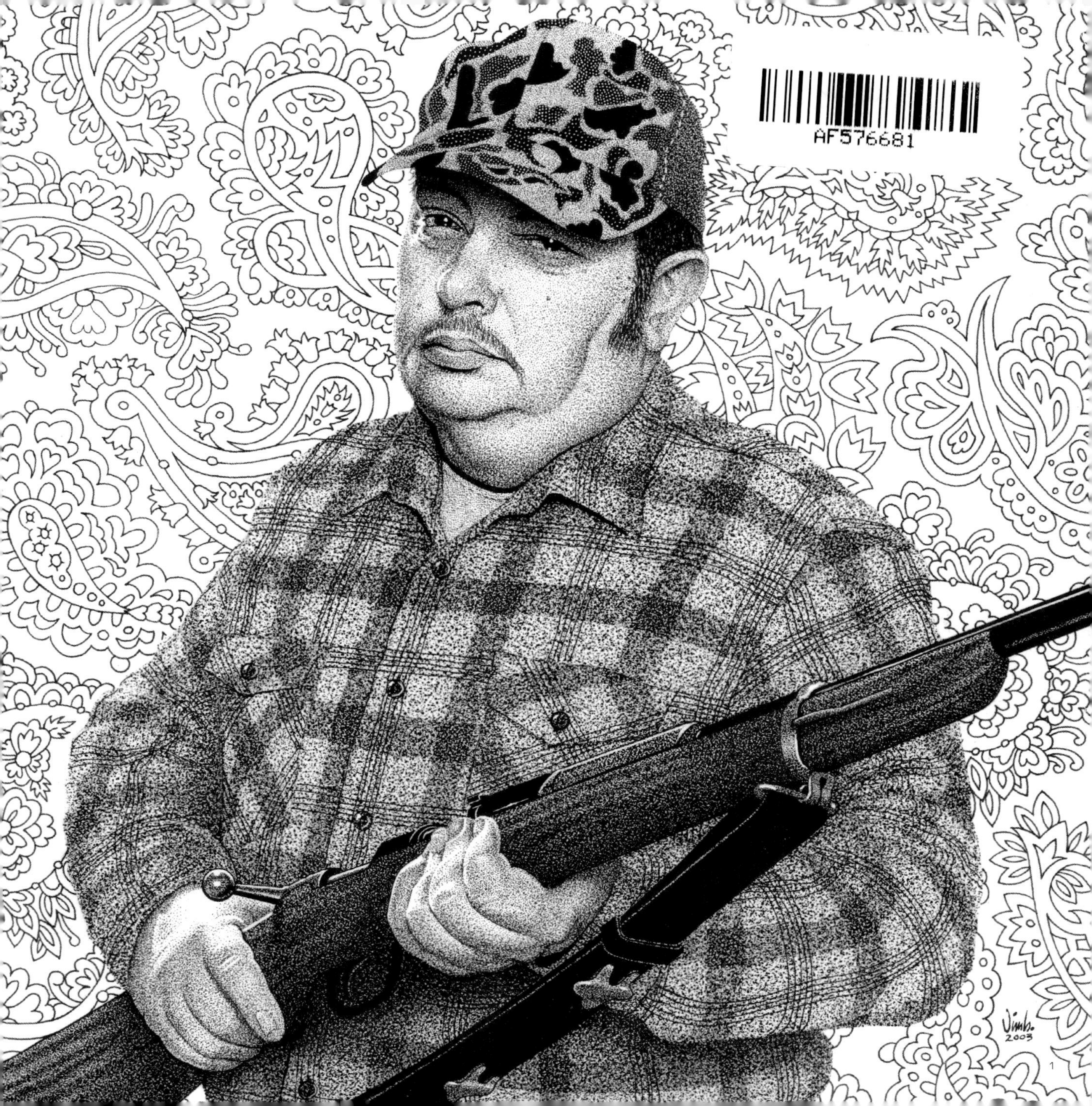

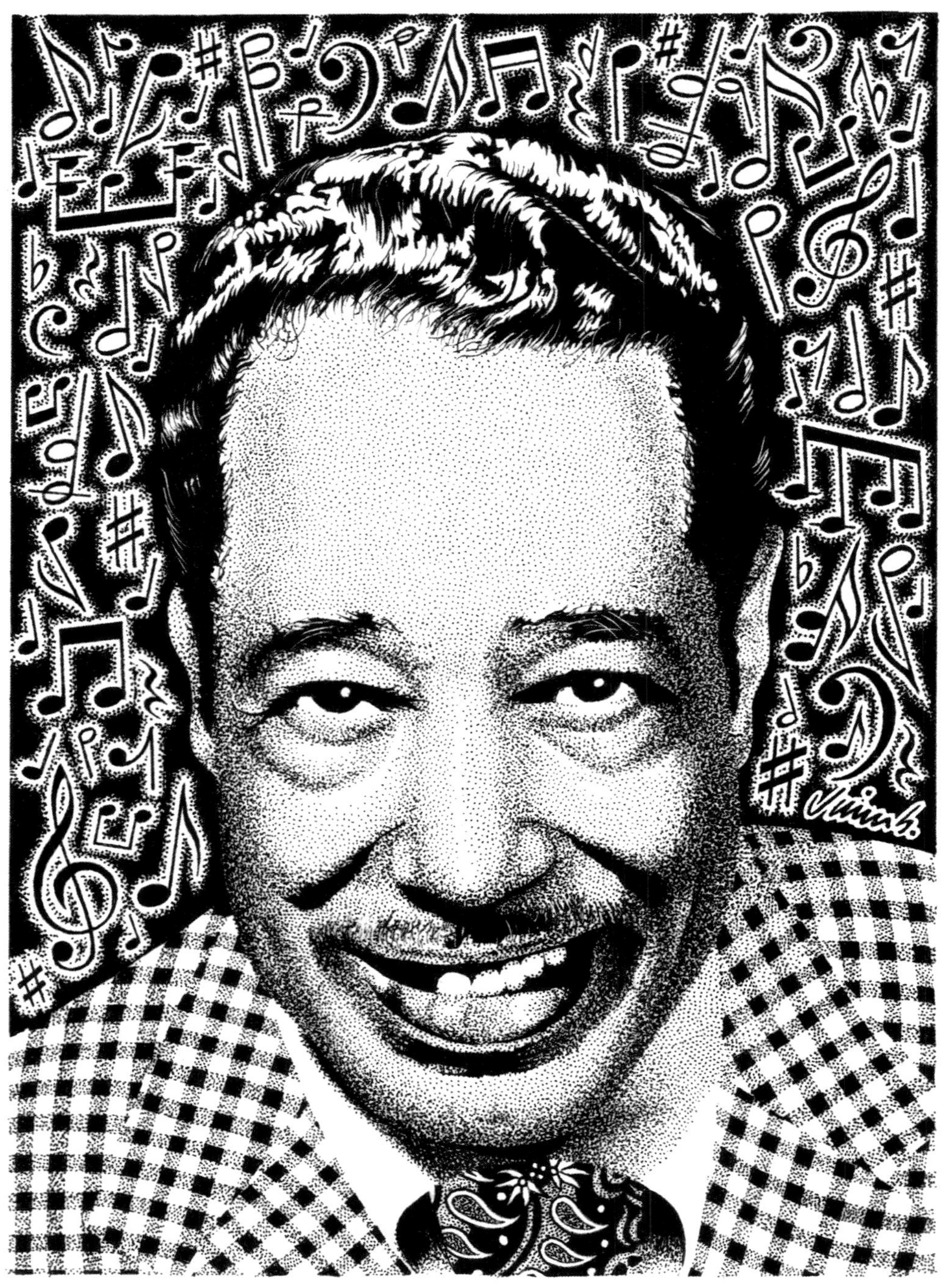

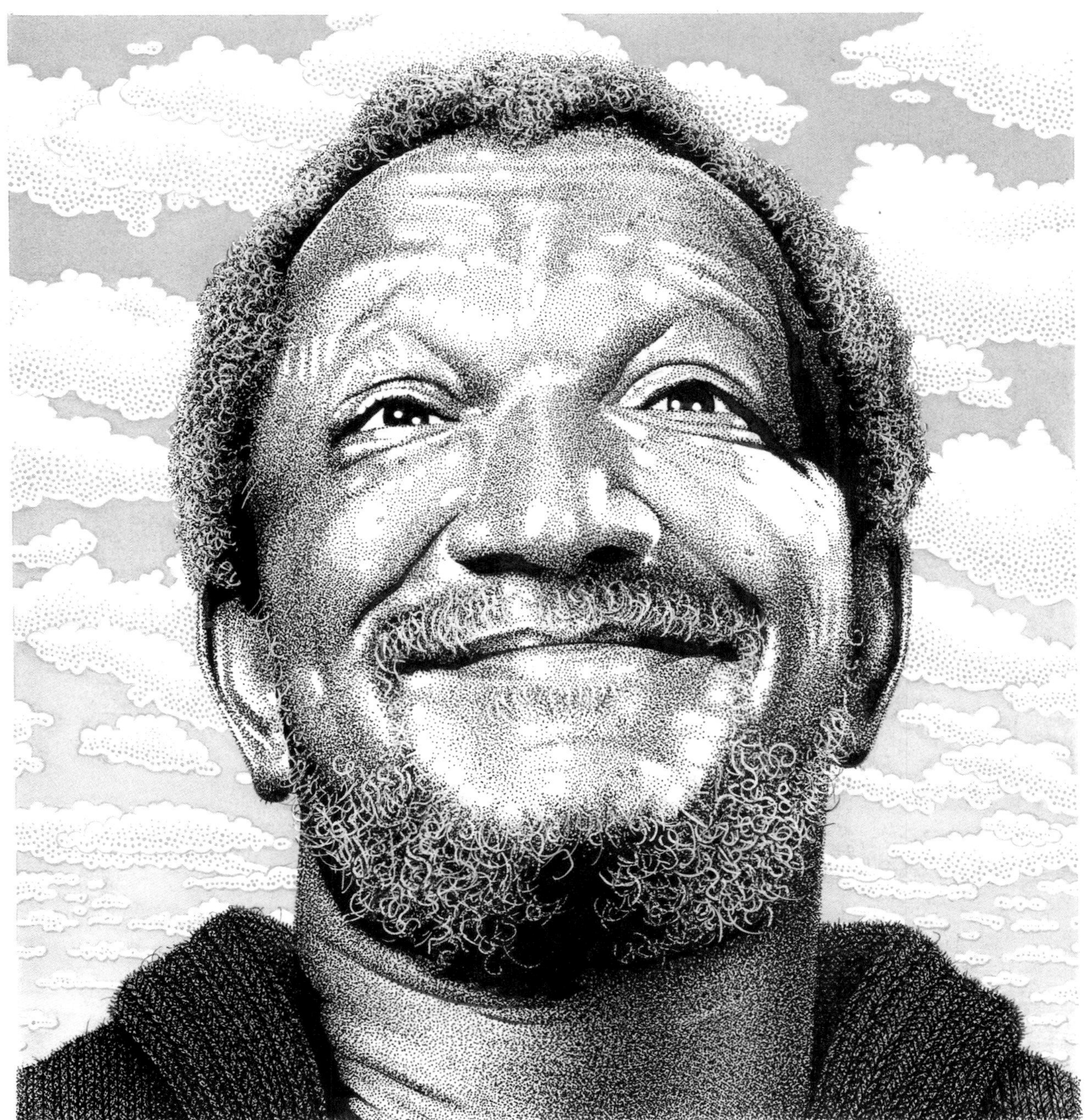

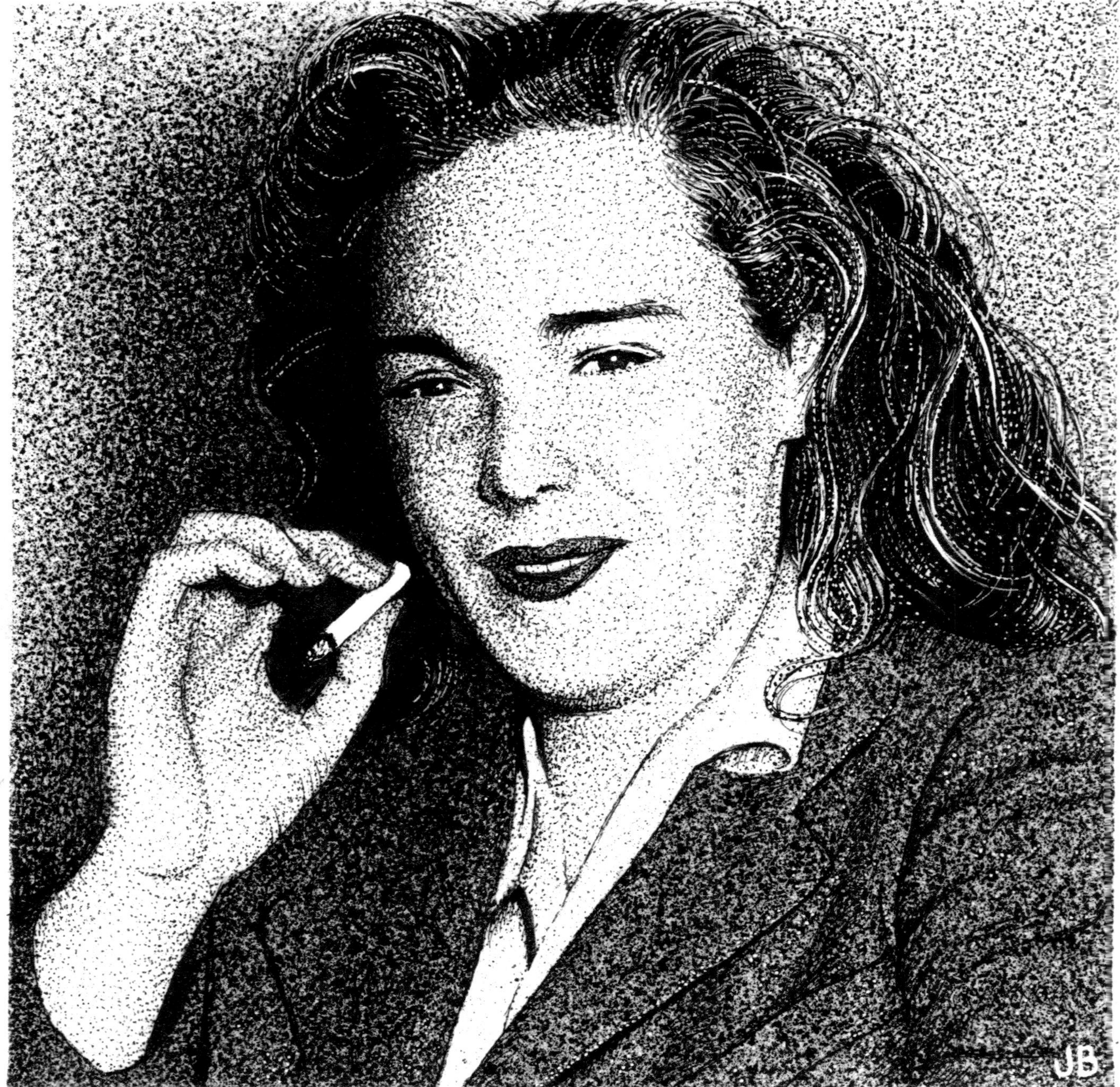

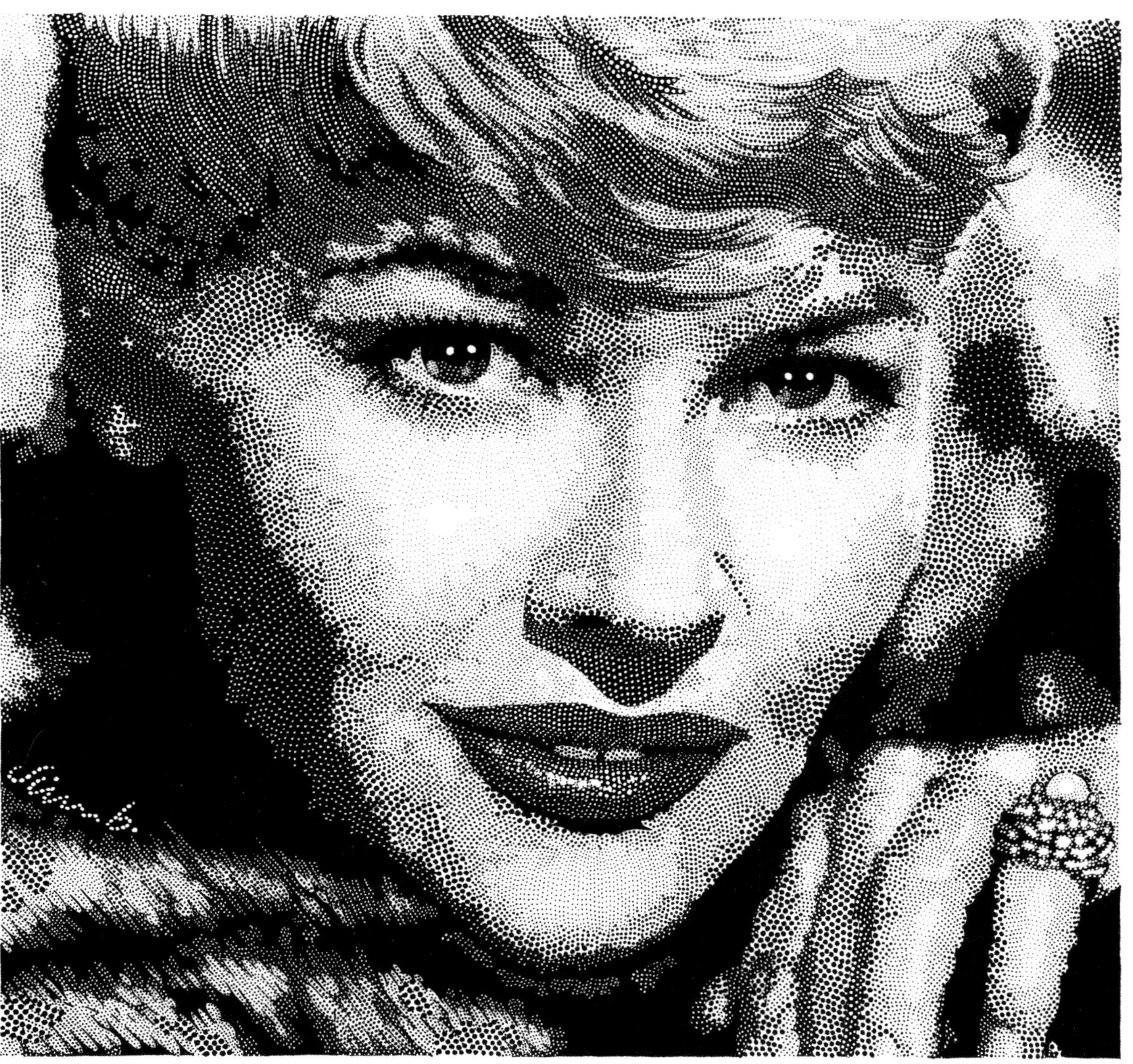

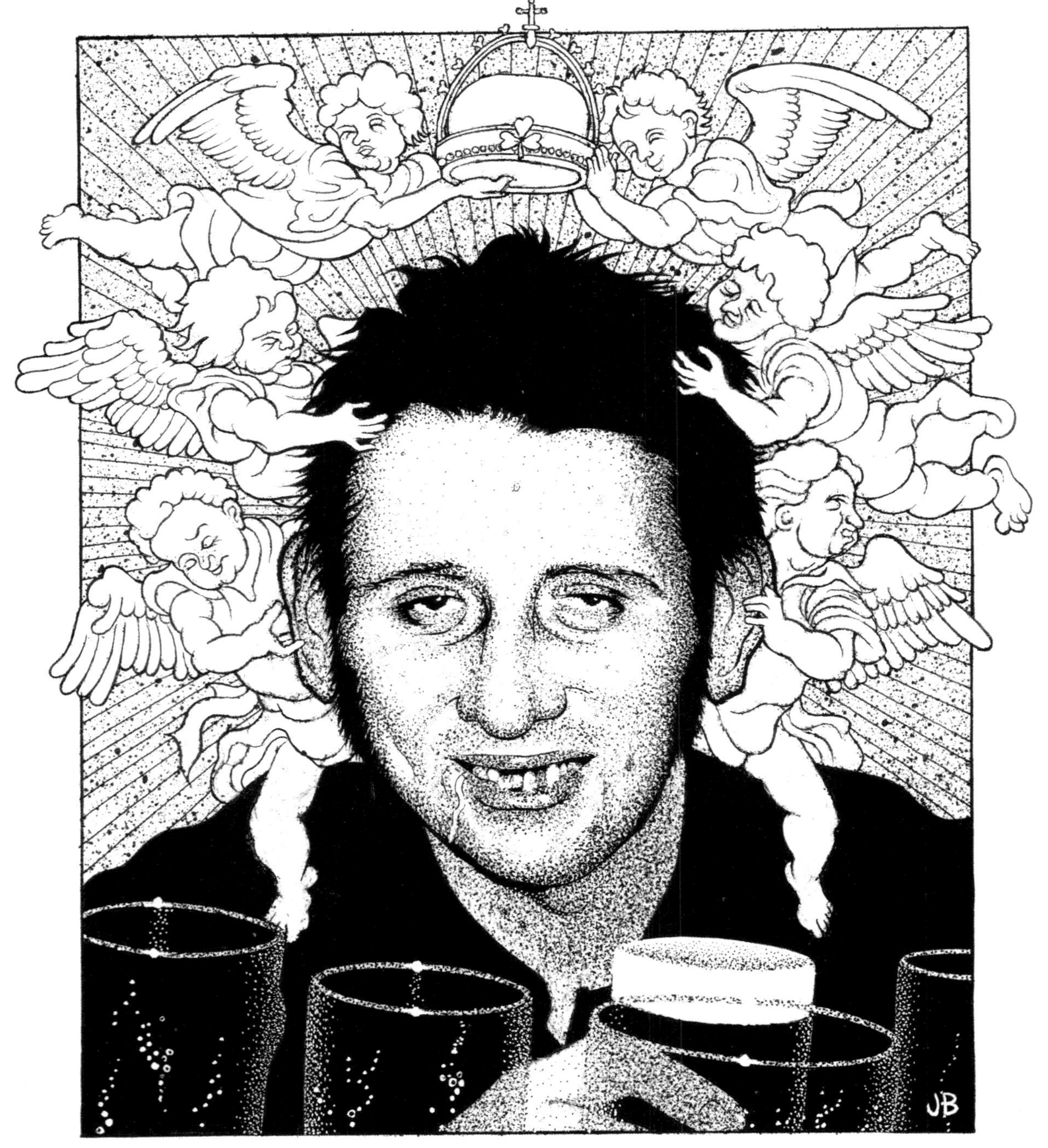
JB

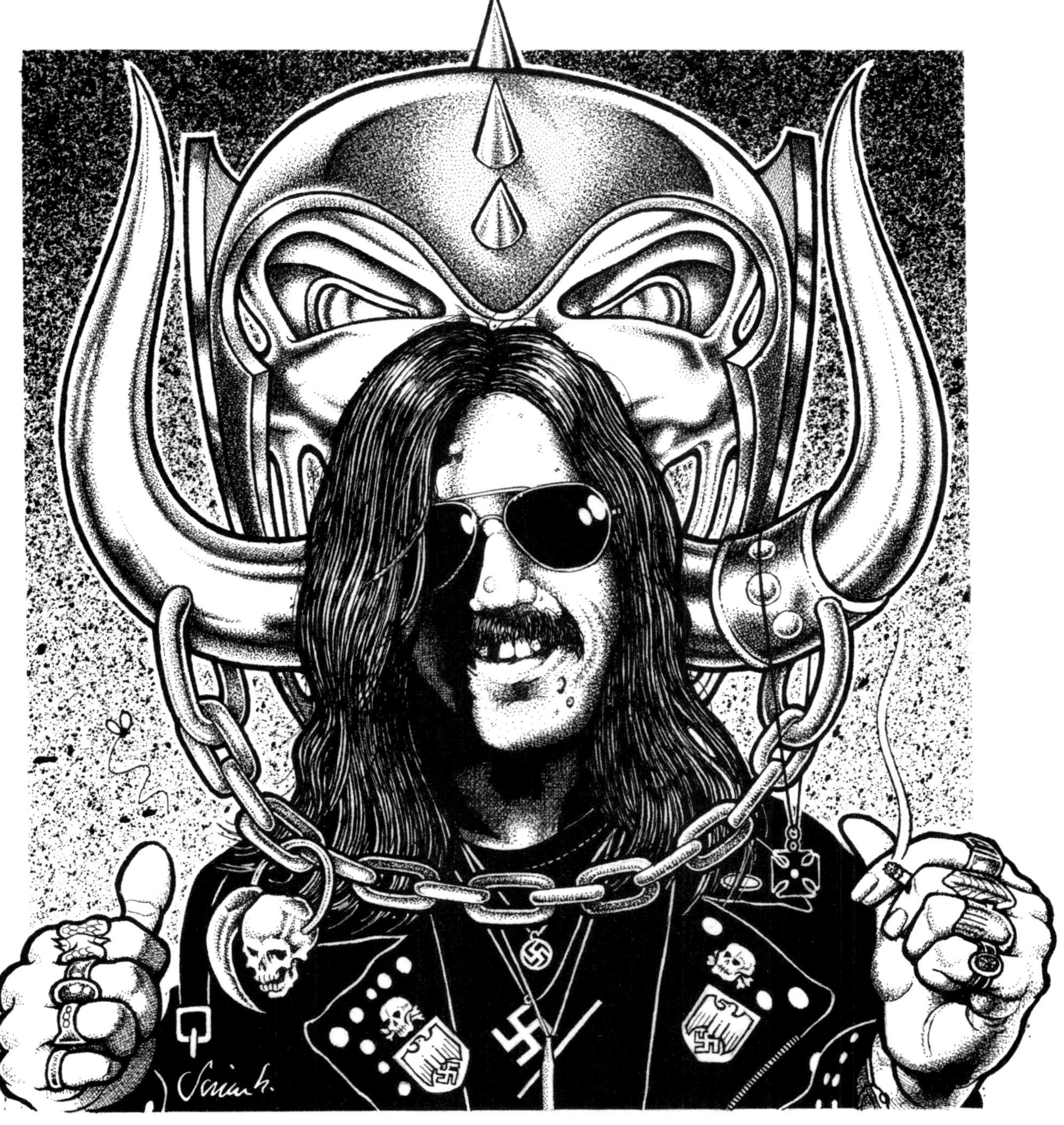

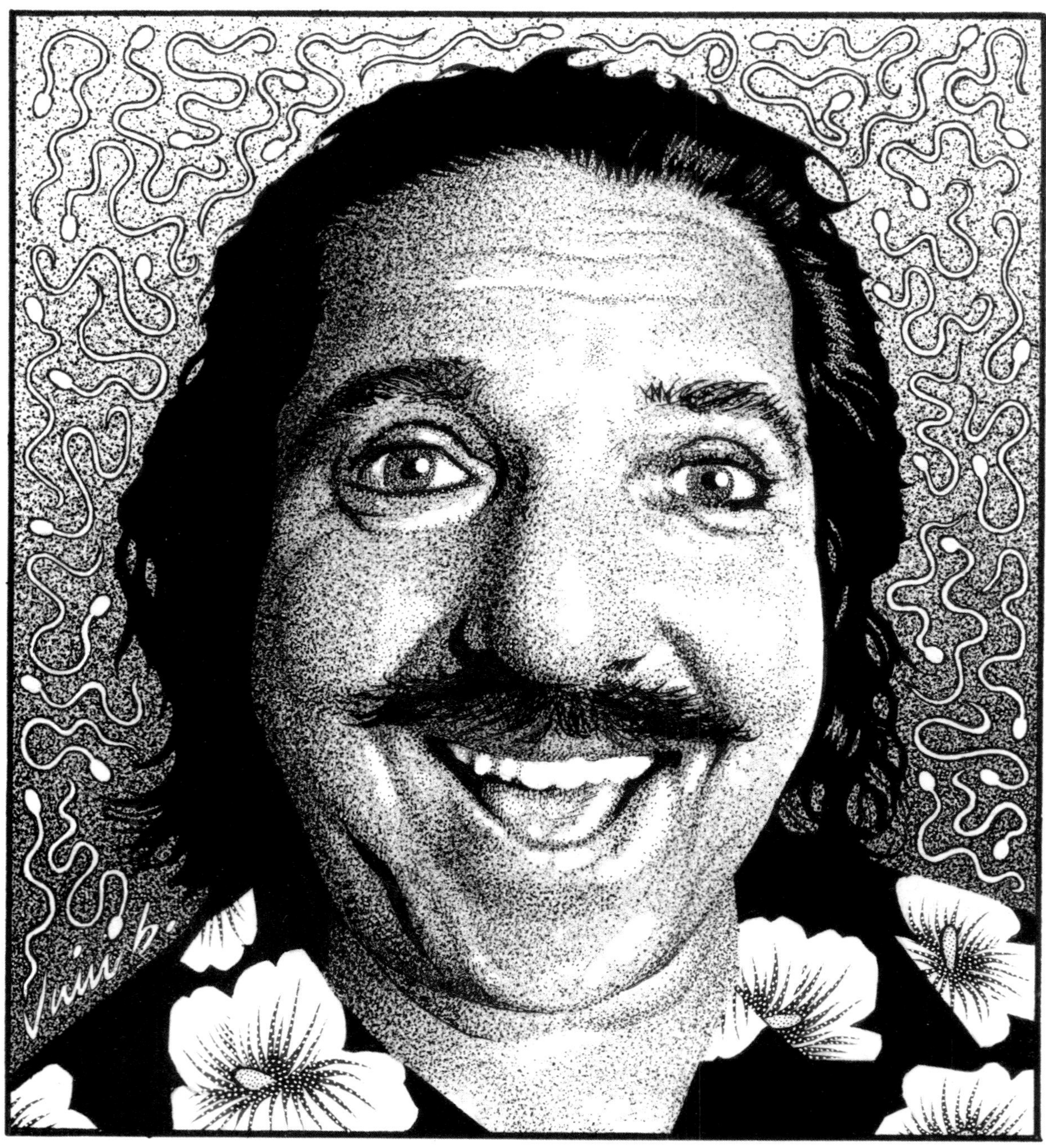

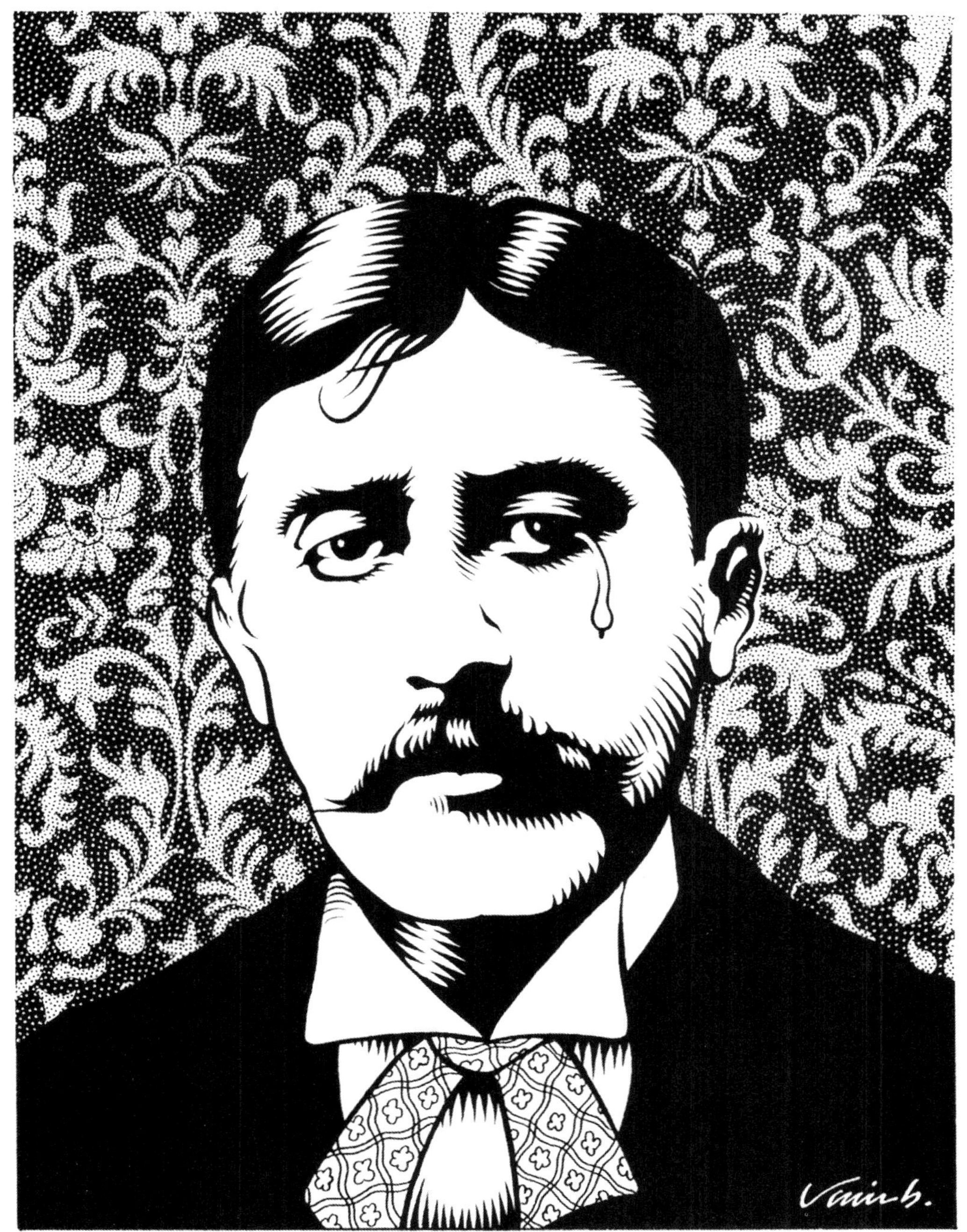

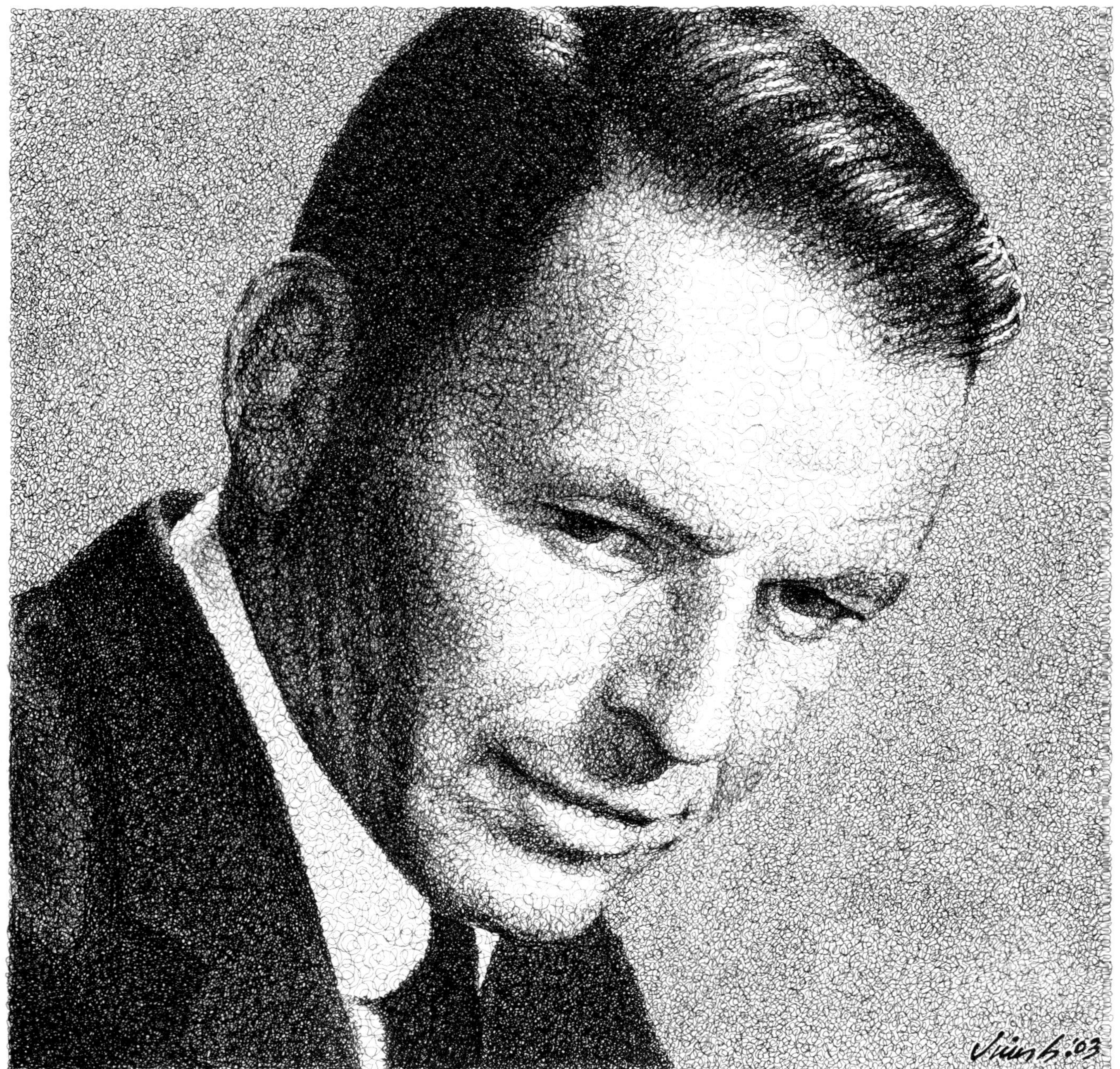

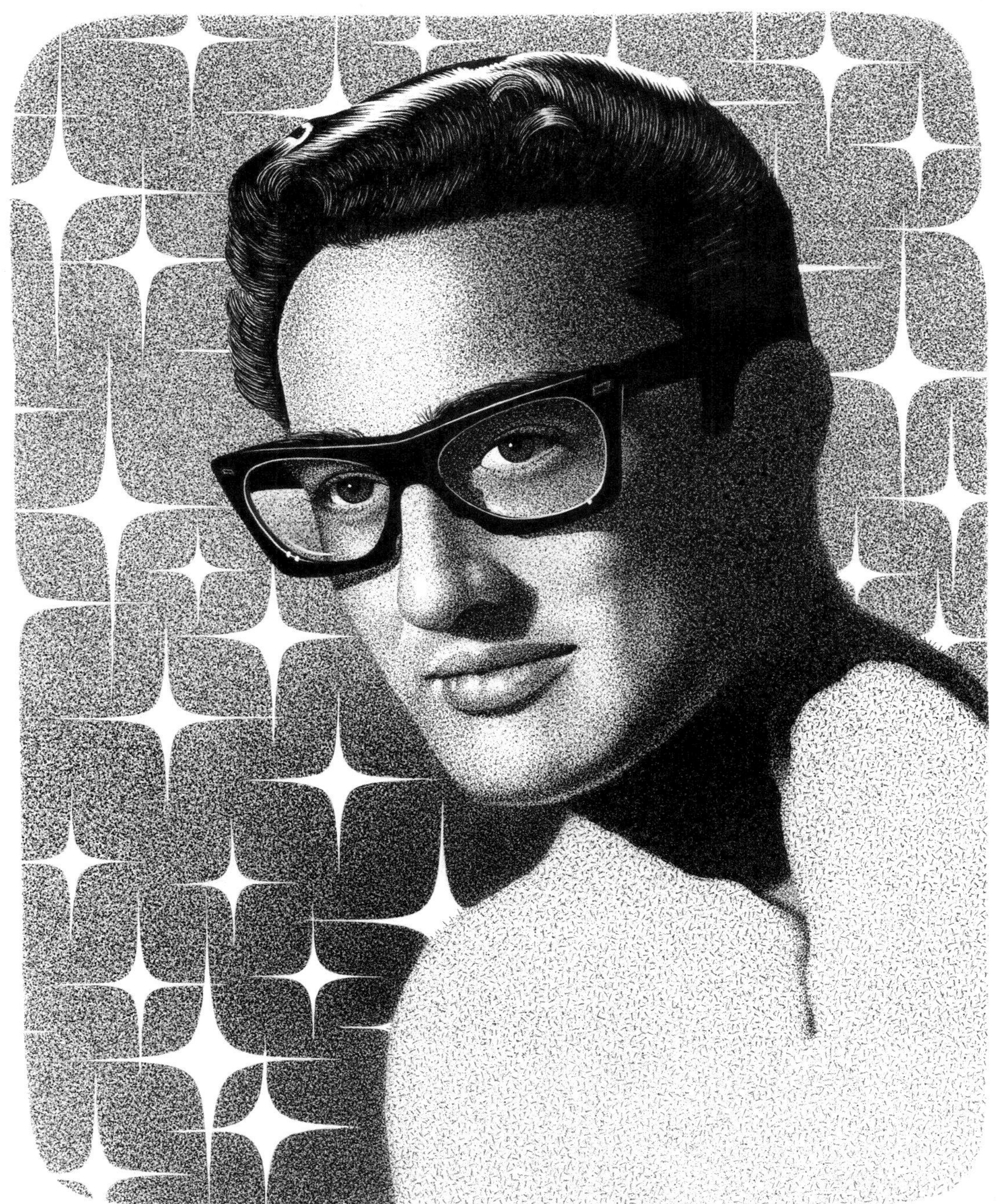

JIM BLANCHARD ©2005

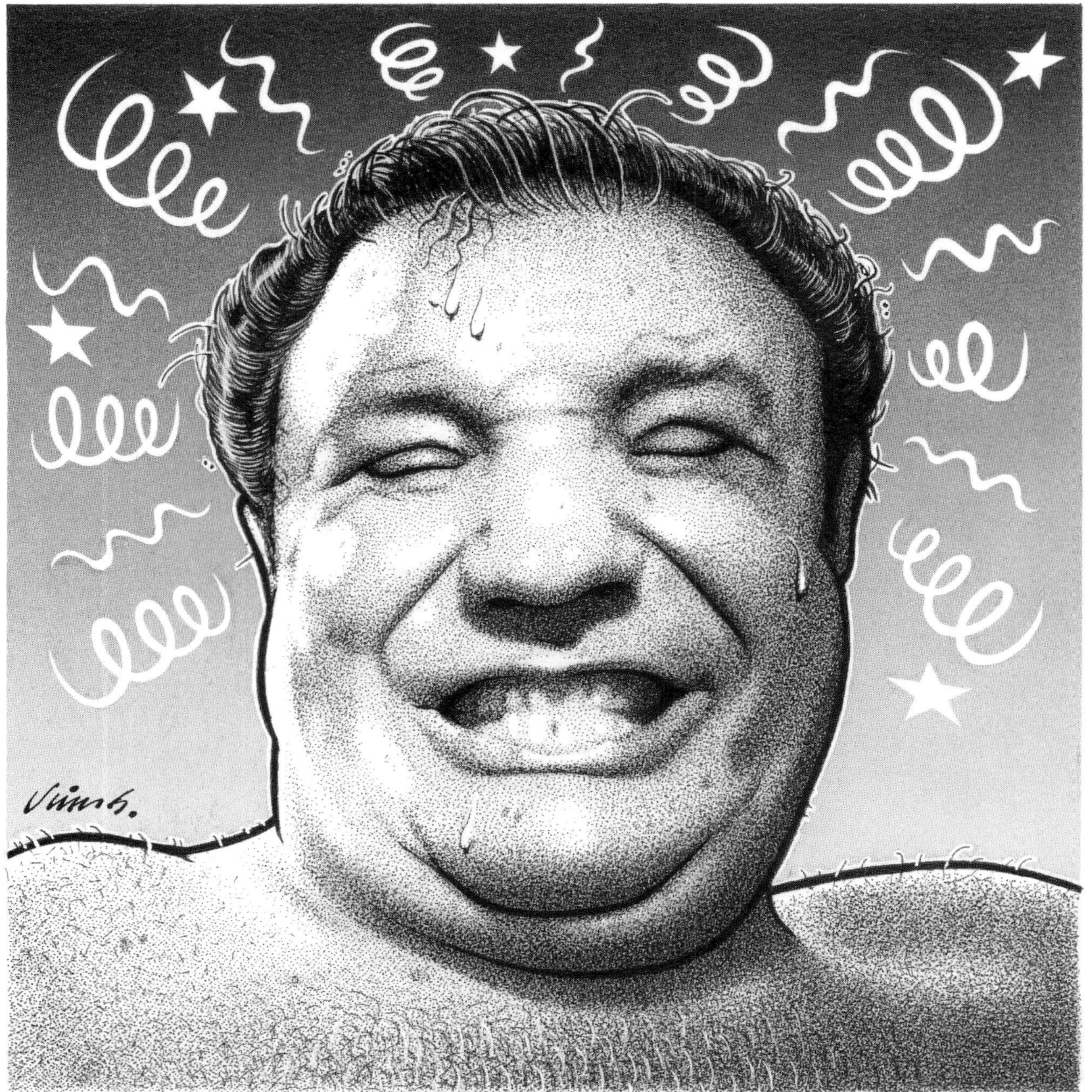

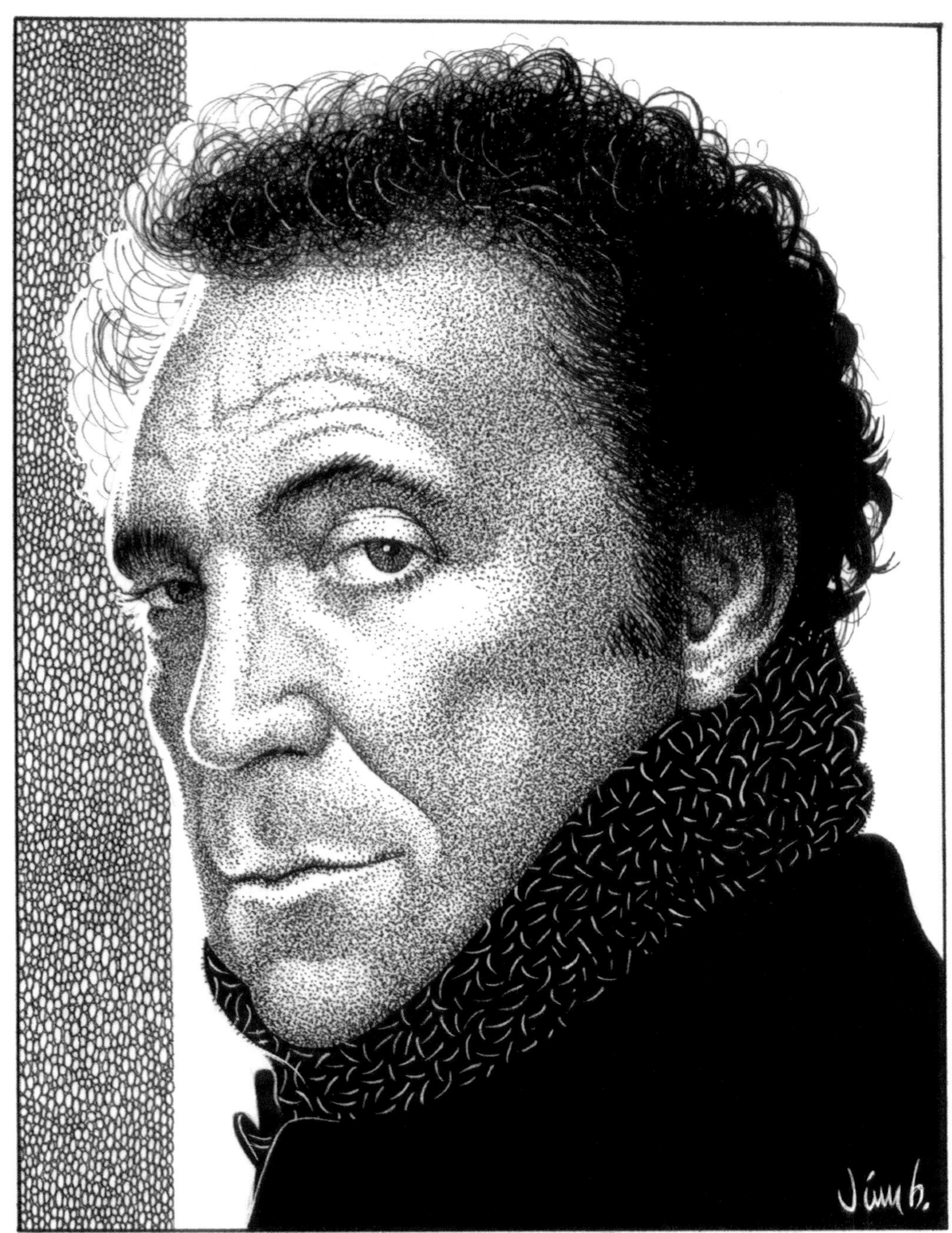

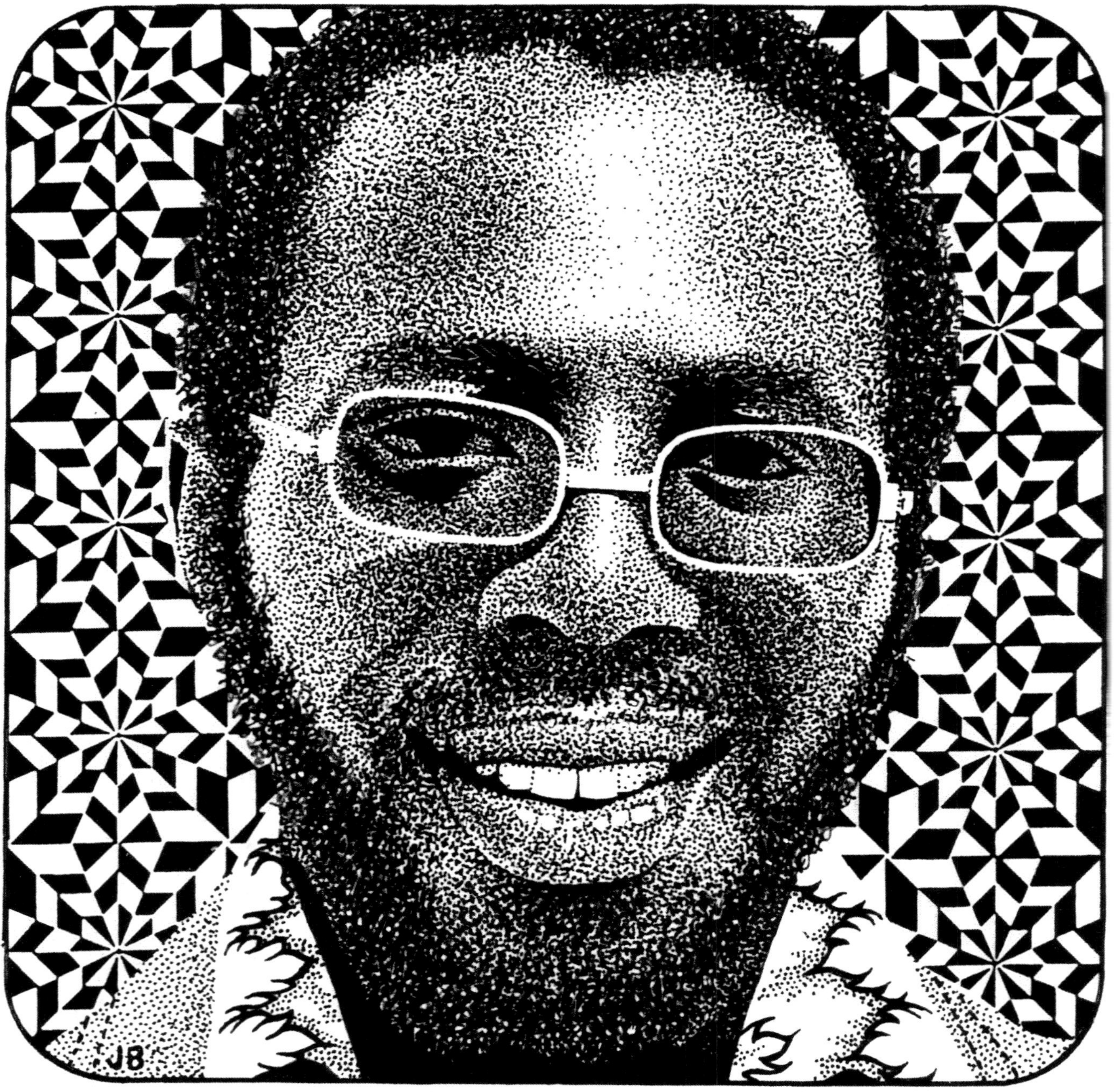
JB

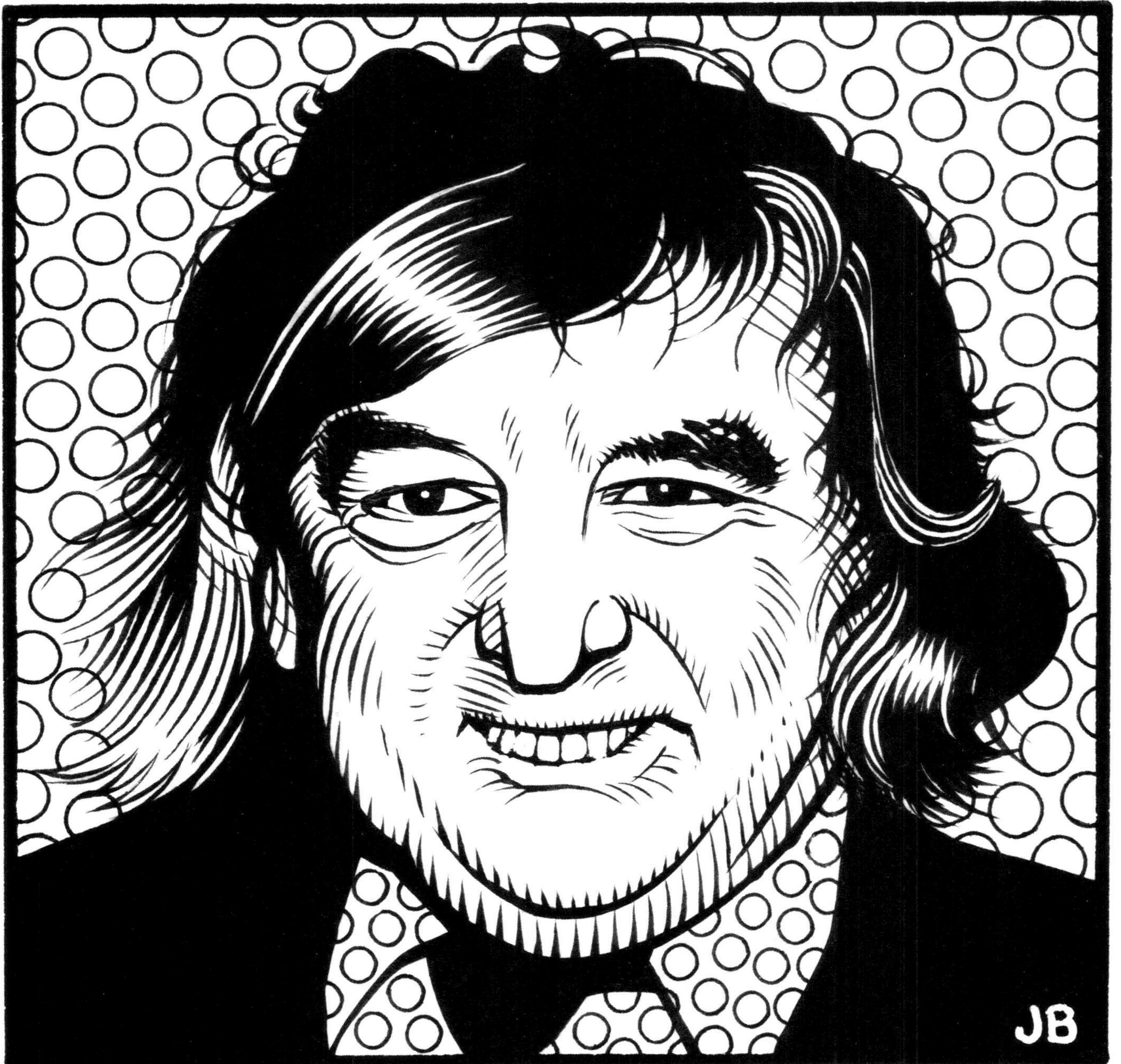
JB

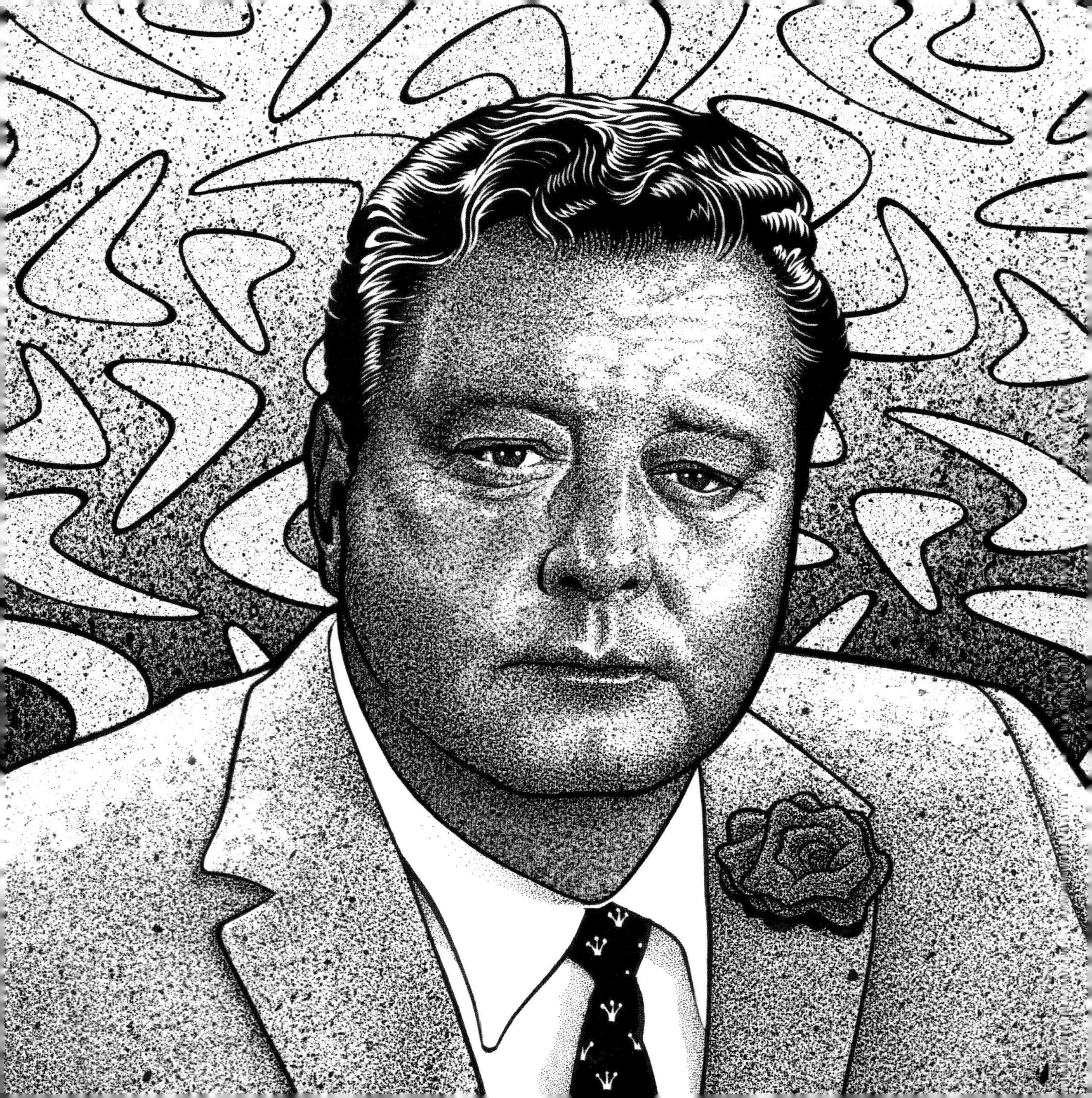

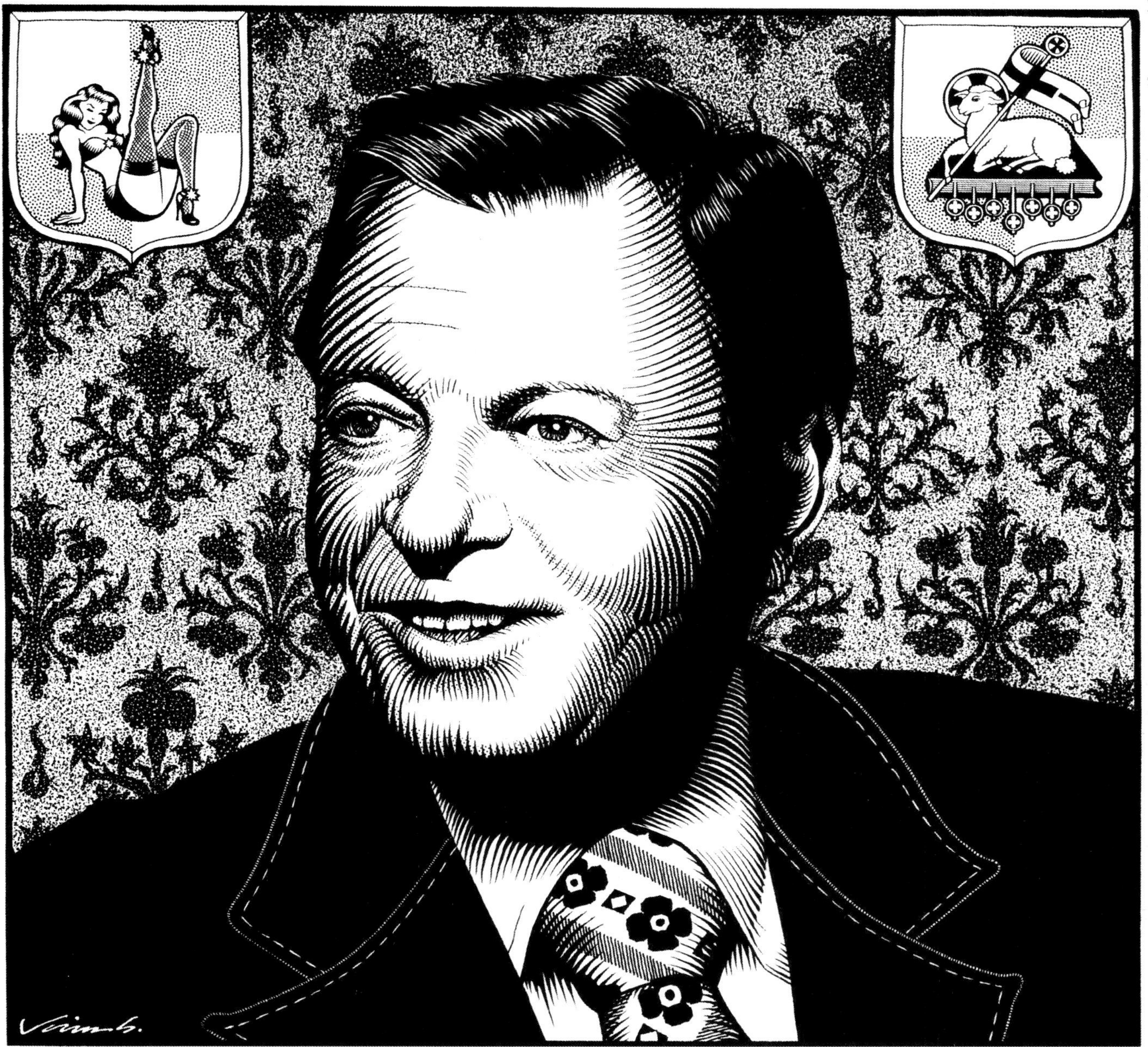

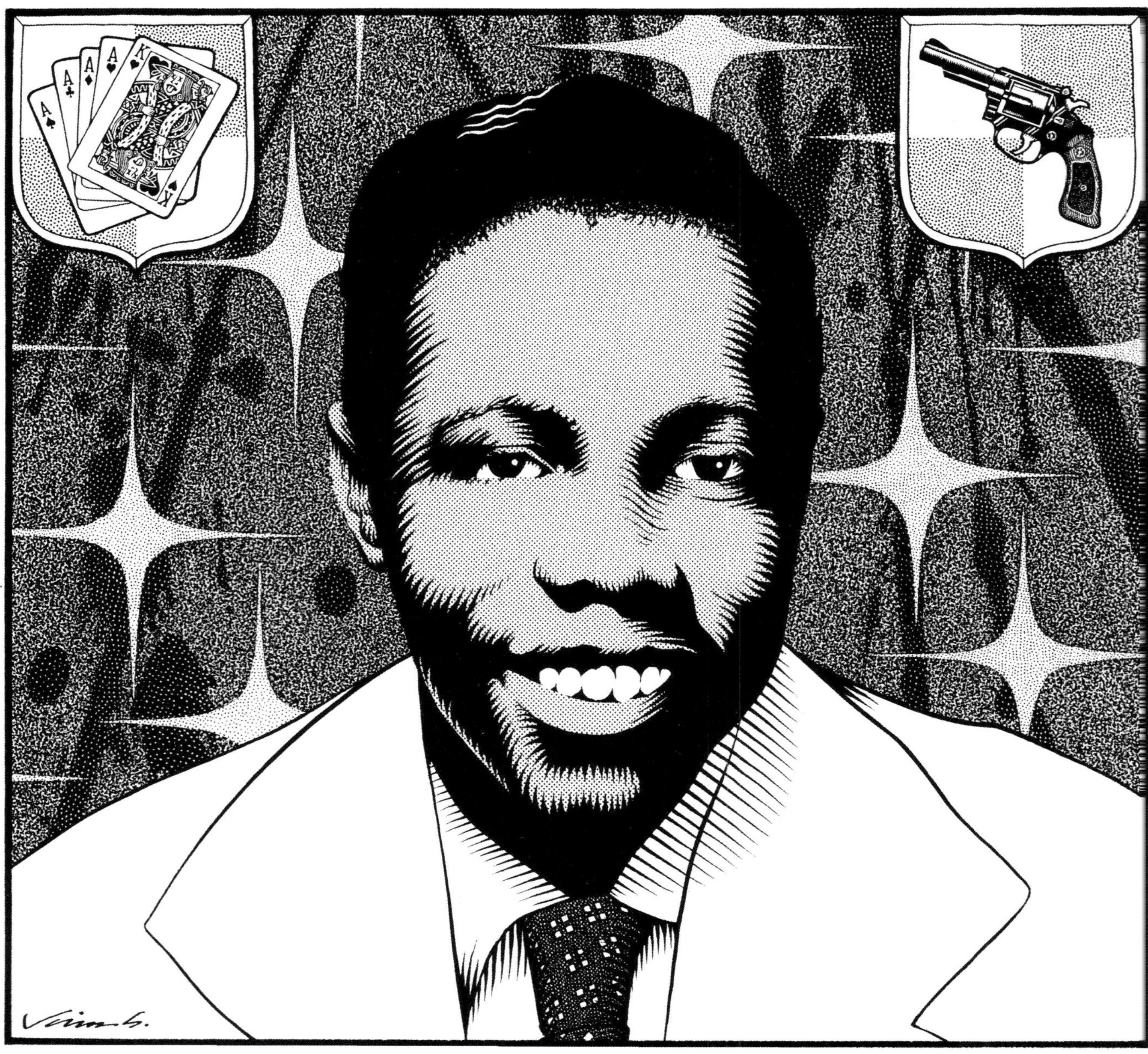

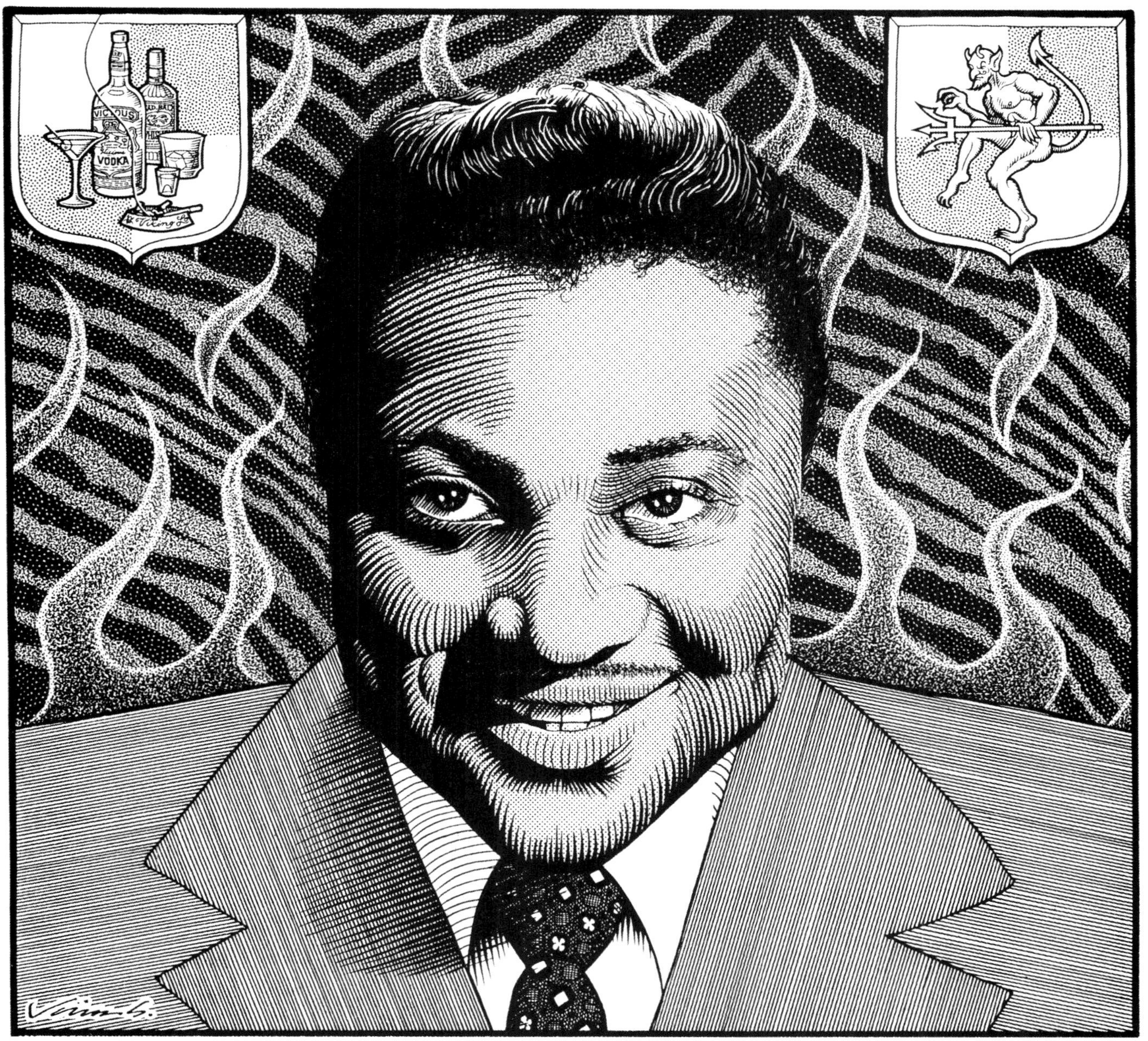
VICIOUS
VODKA

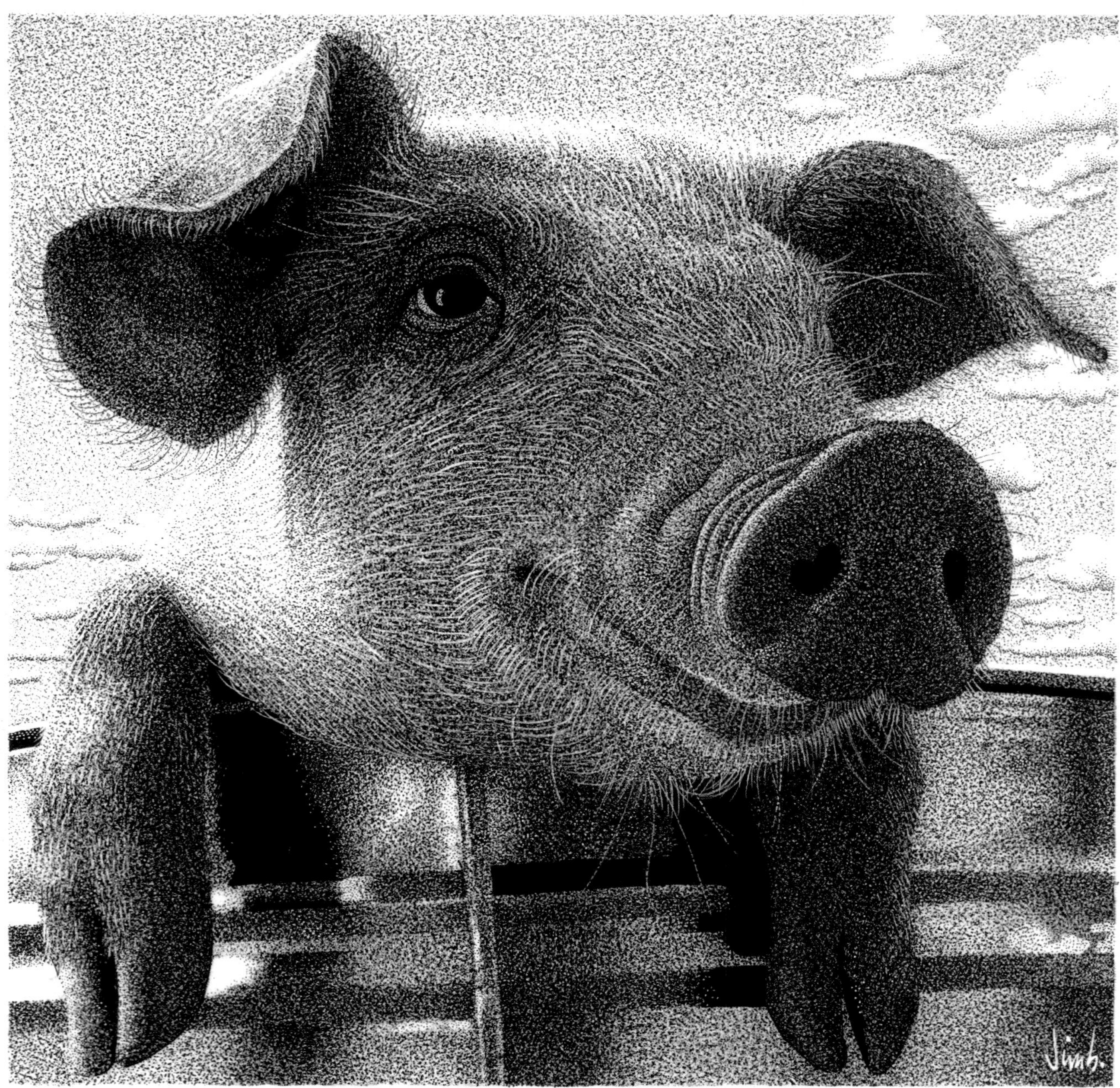

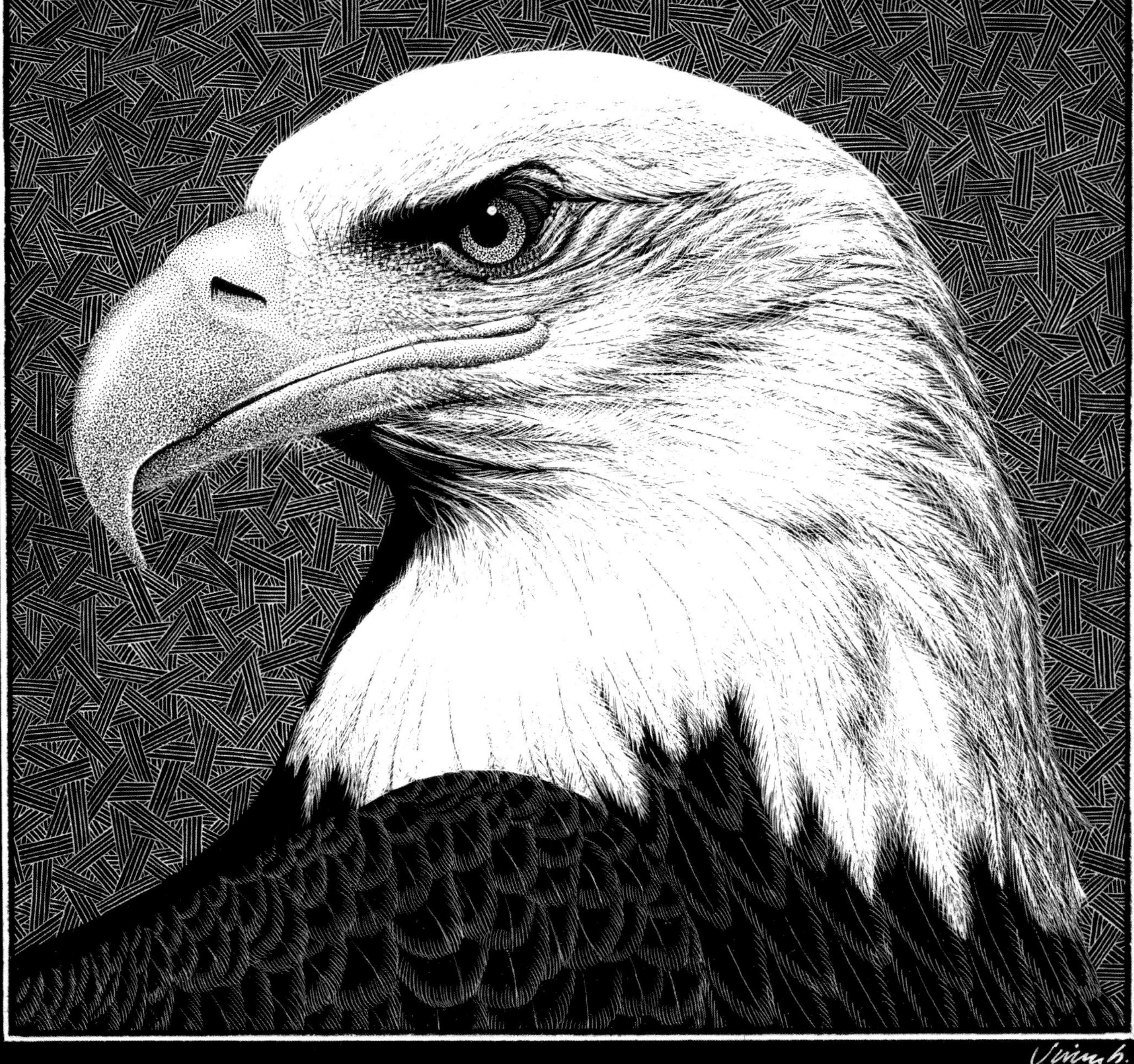

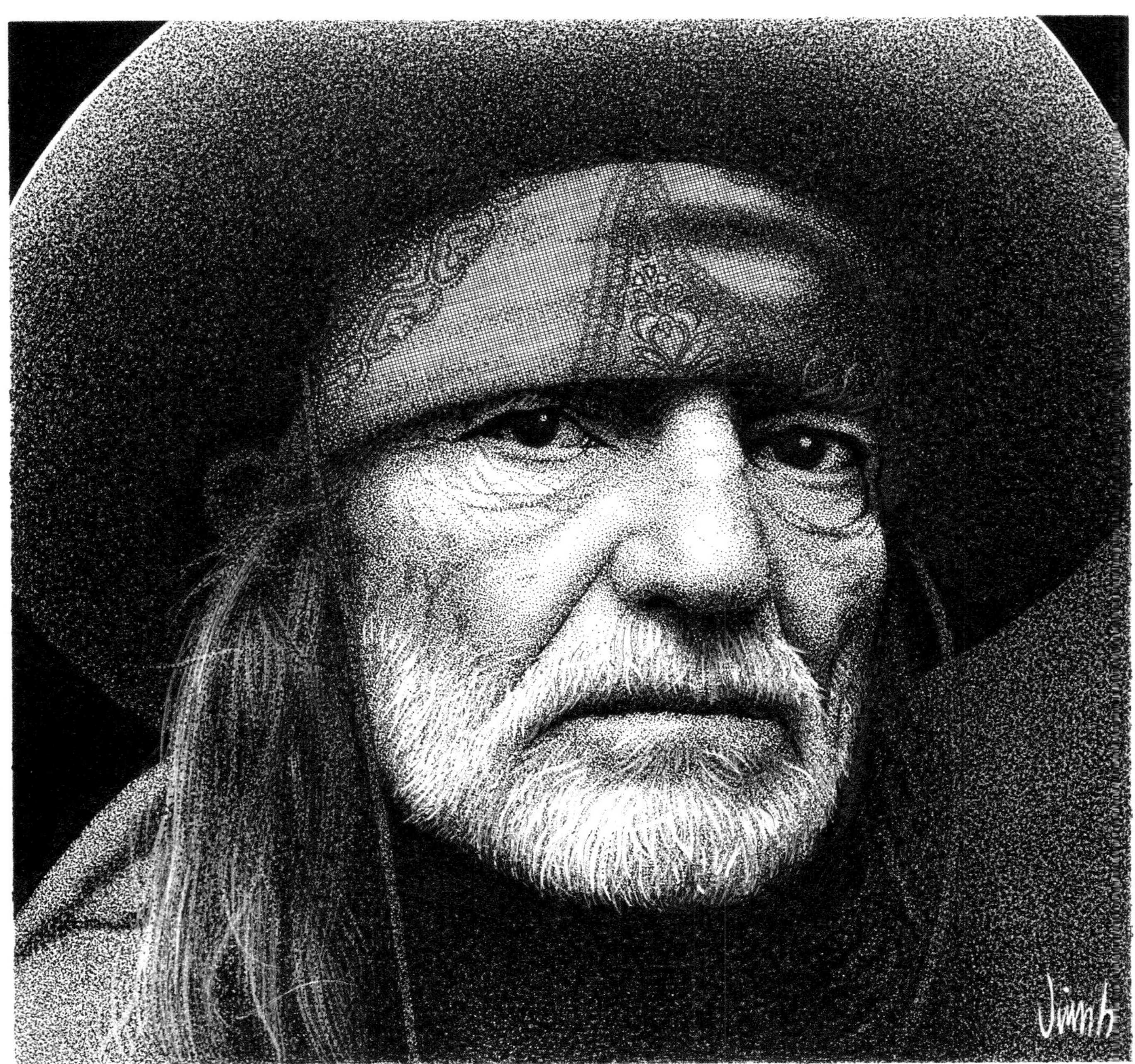
Jim h

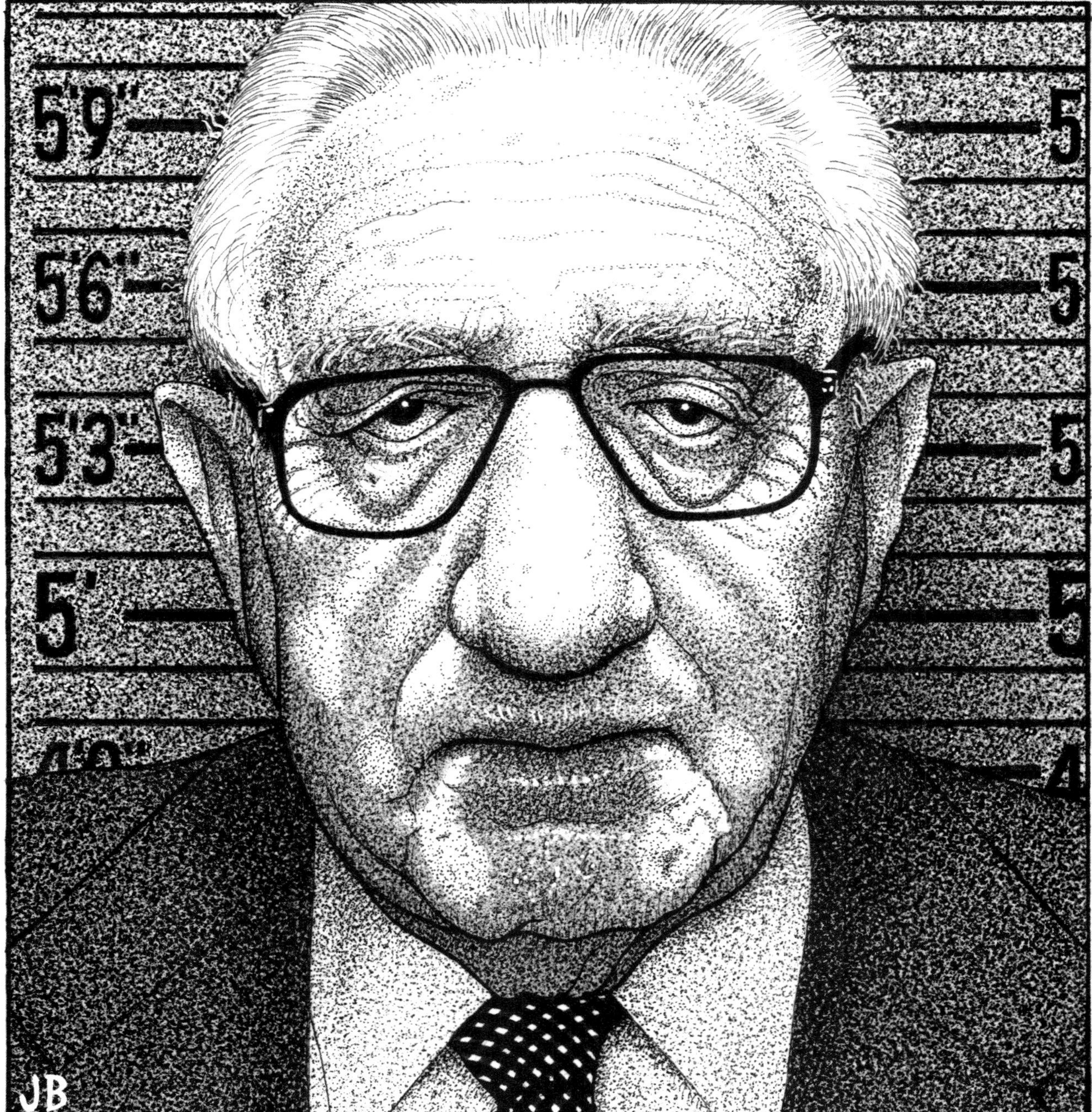
5'9"
5'6"
5'3"
5'
JB

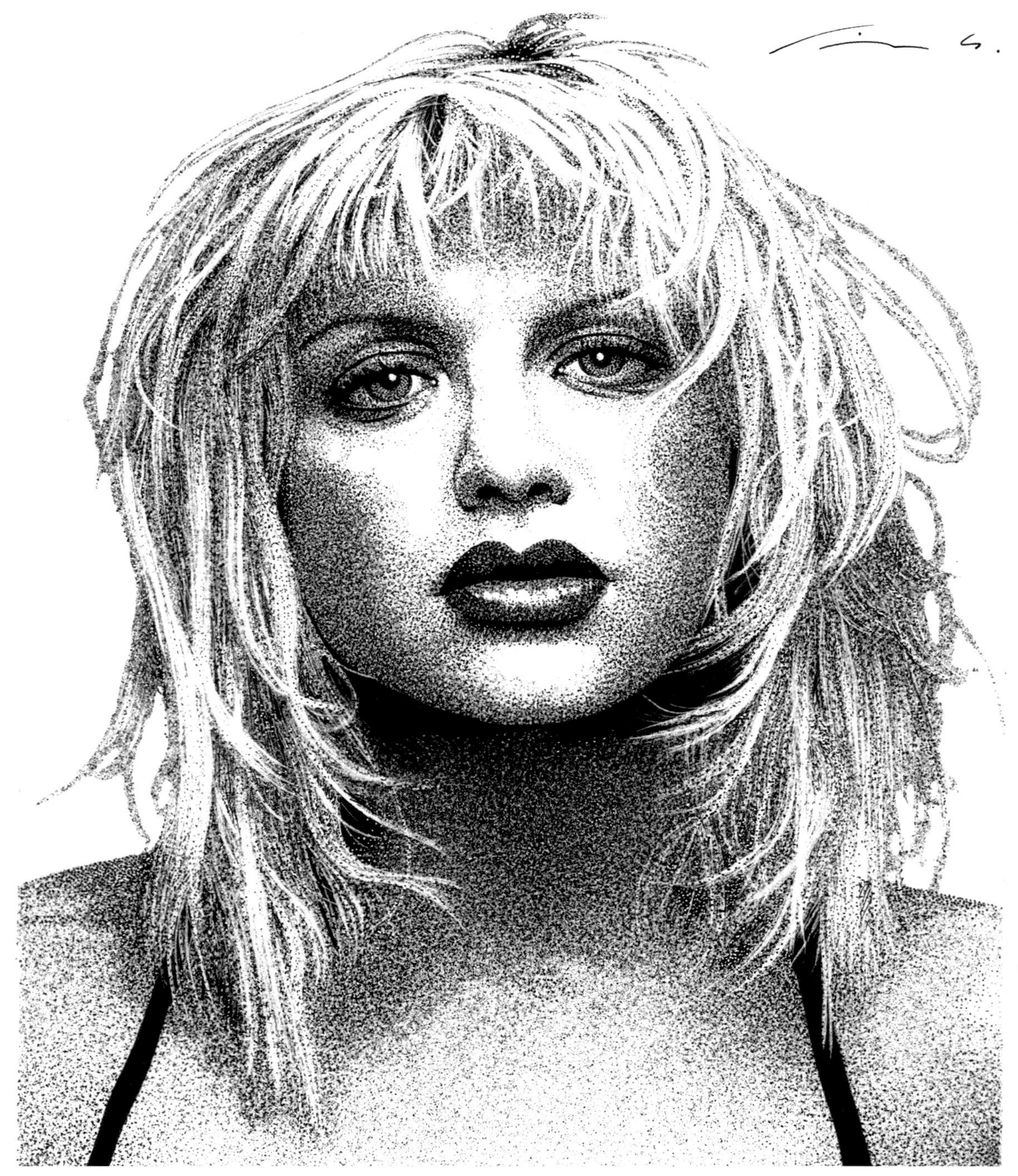

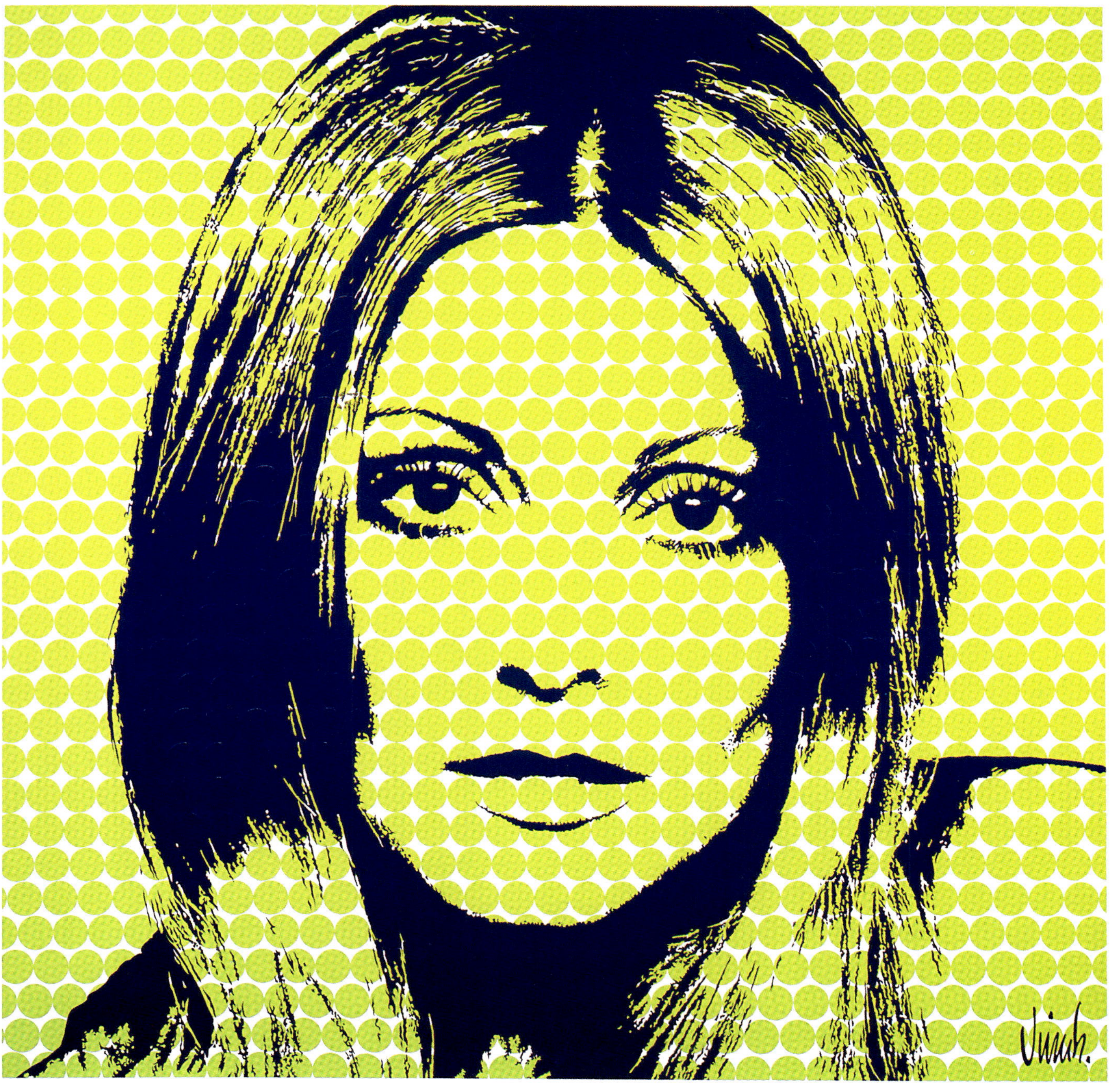

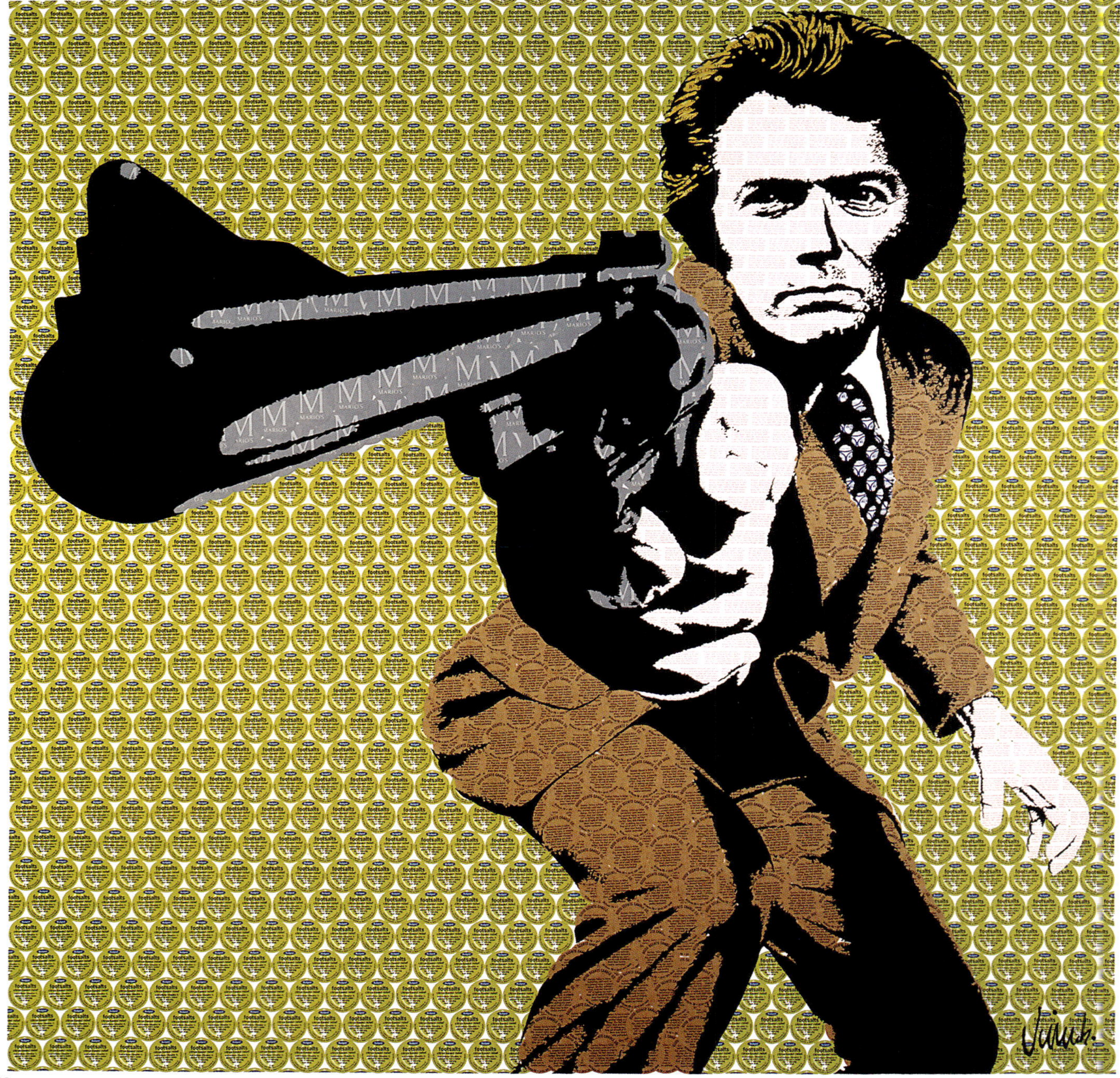
footsalts
MARIO'S

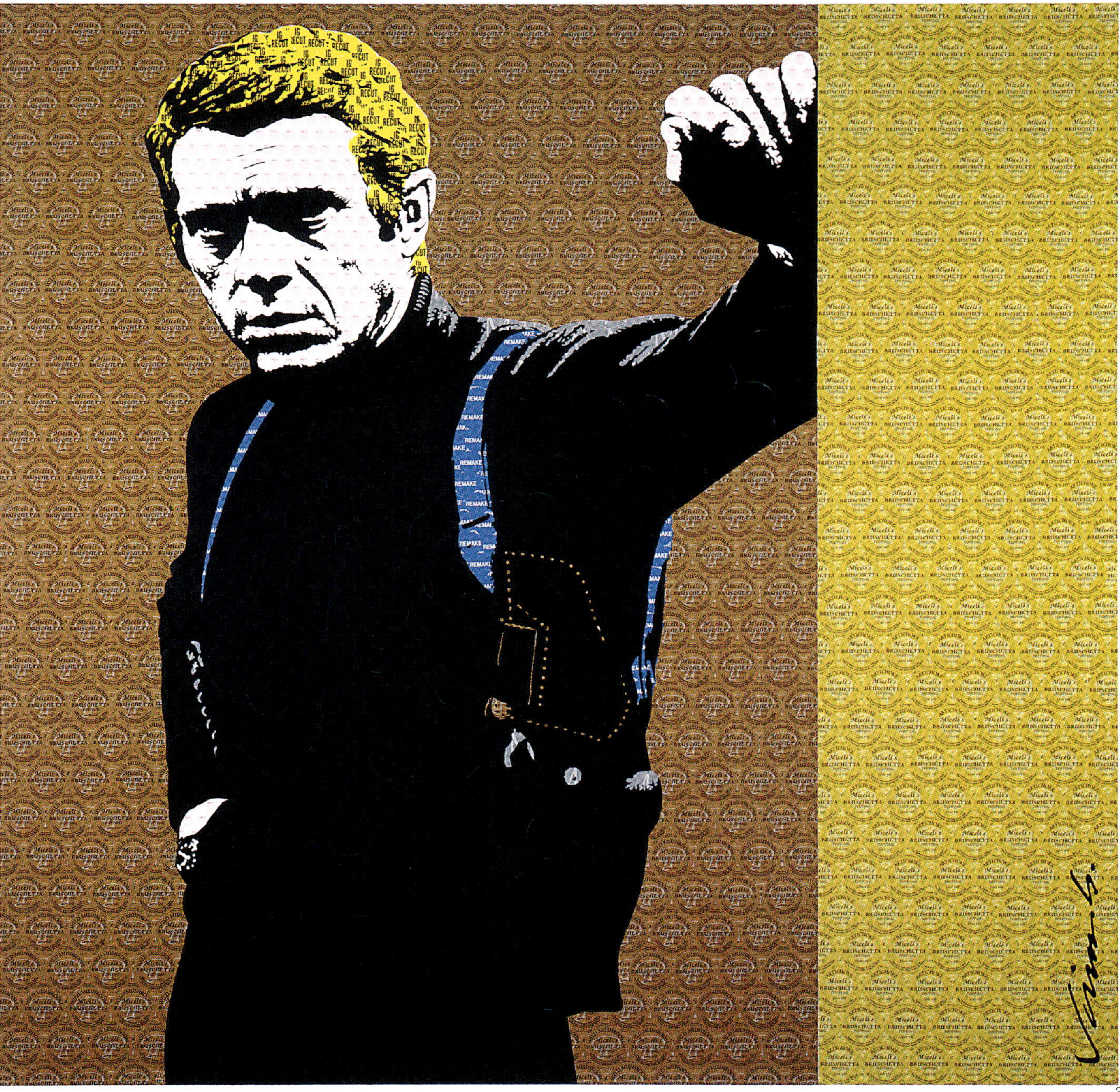
RECUT
REMAKE
Miceli's
BRUSCHETTA

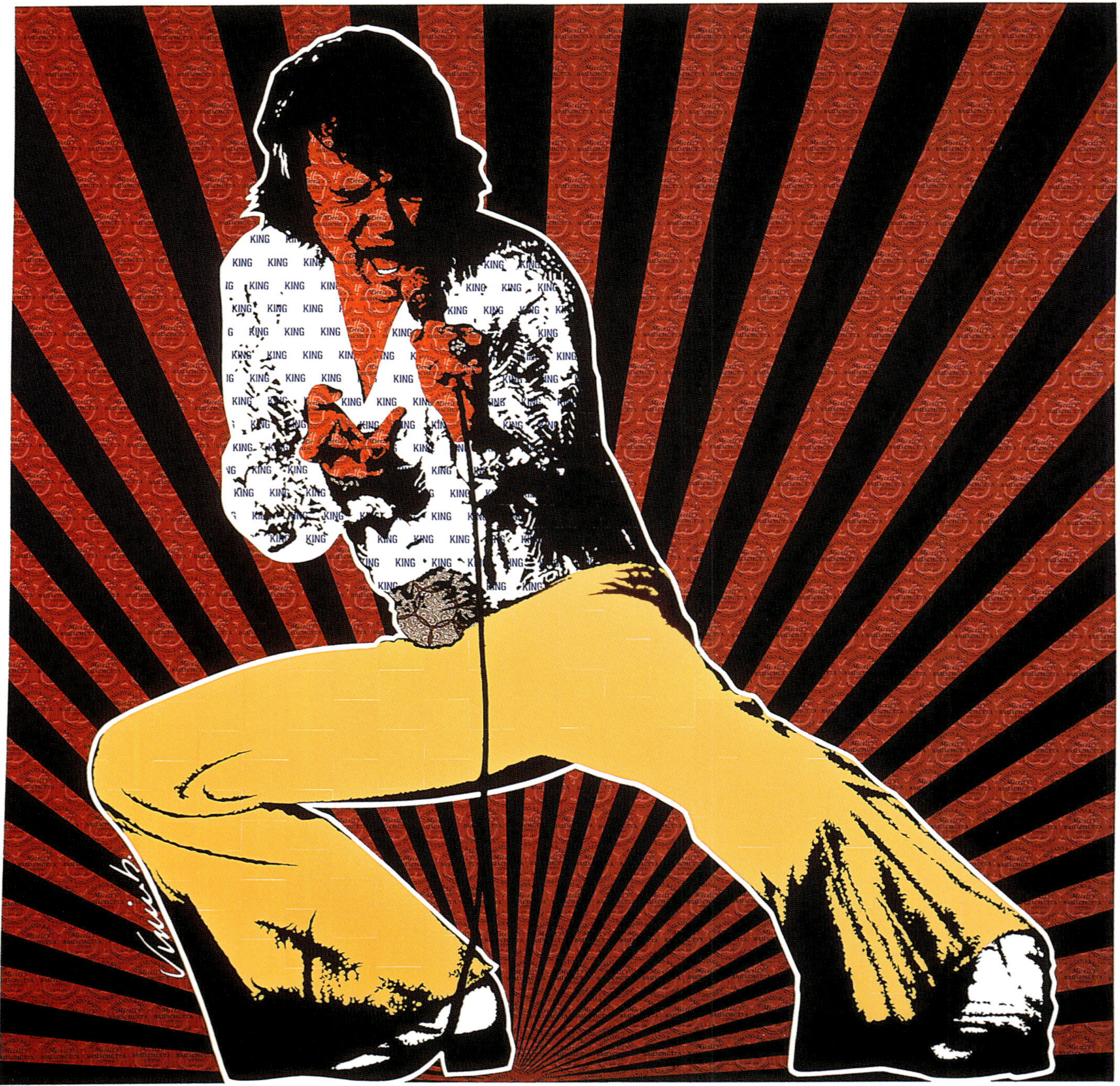
KING

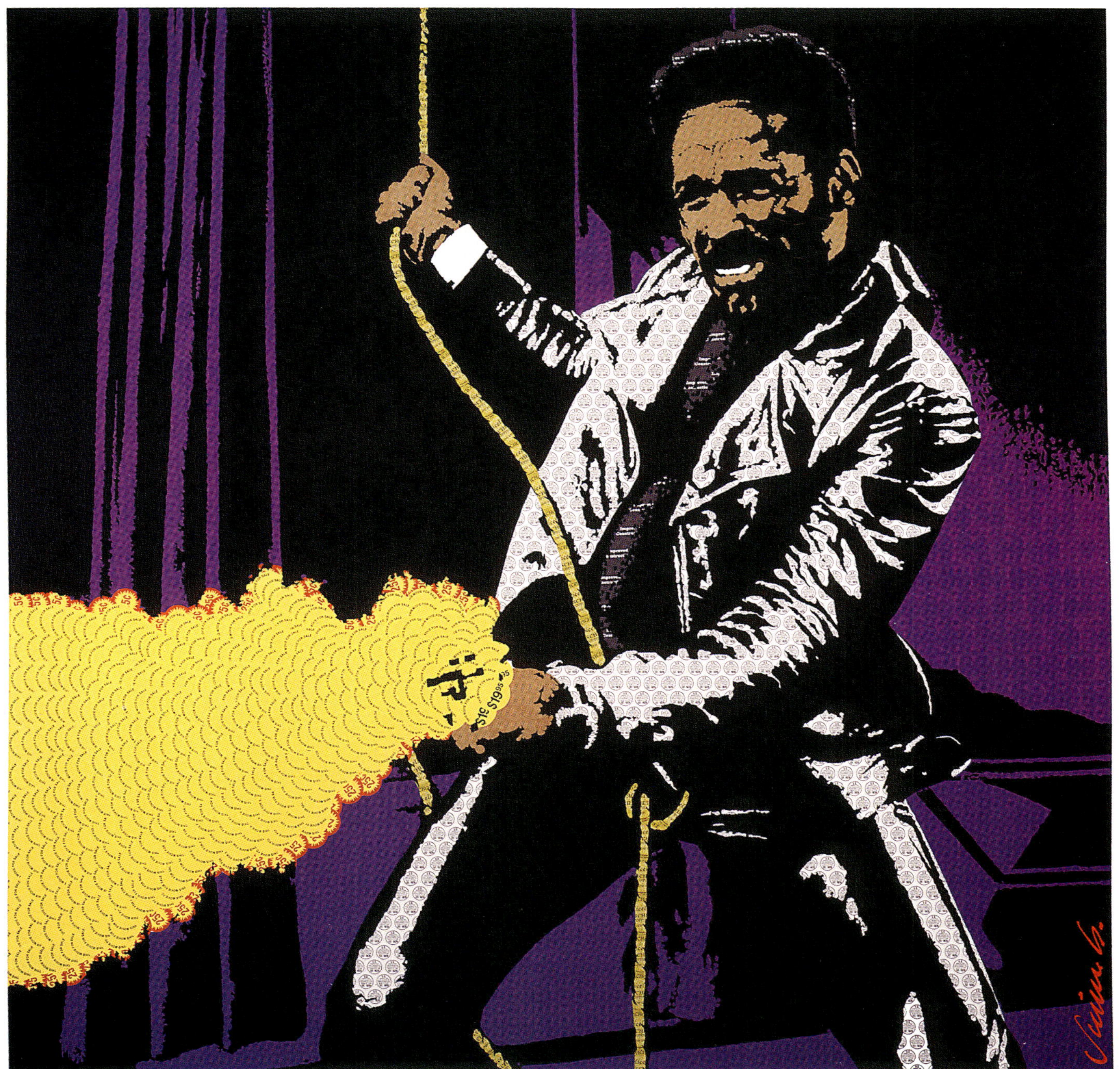

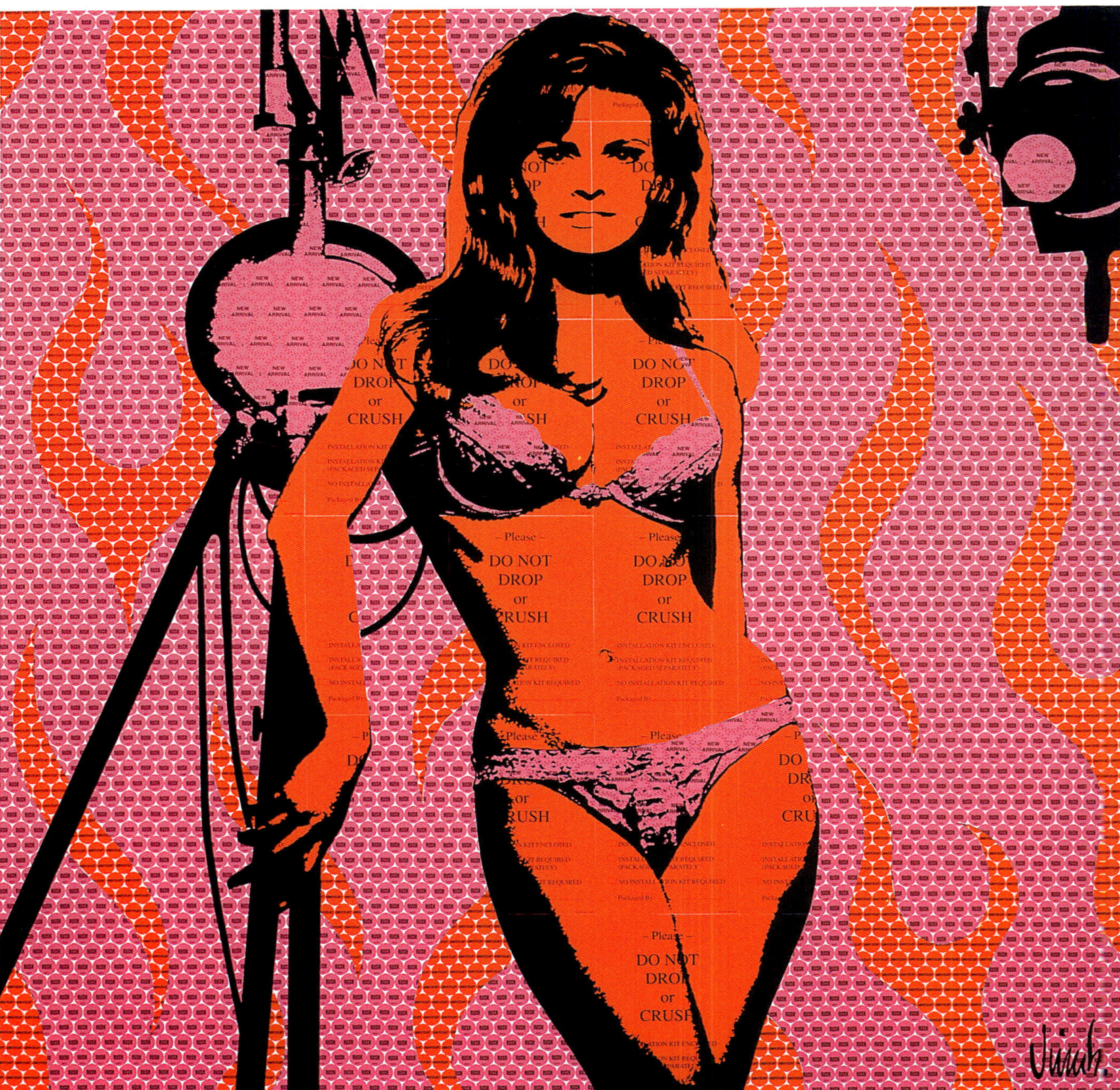
– Please –
DO NOT
DROP
or
CRUSH
INSTALLATION KIT ENCLOSED
INSTALLATION KIT REQUIRED
(PACKAGED SEPARATELY)
NO INSTALLATION KIT REQUIRED
Packaged By
NEW
ARRIVAL

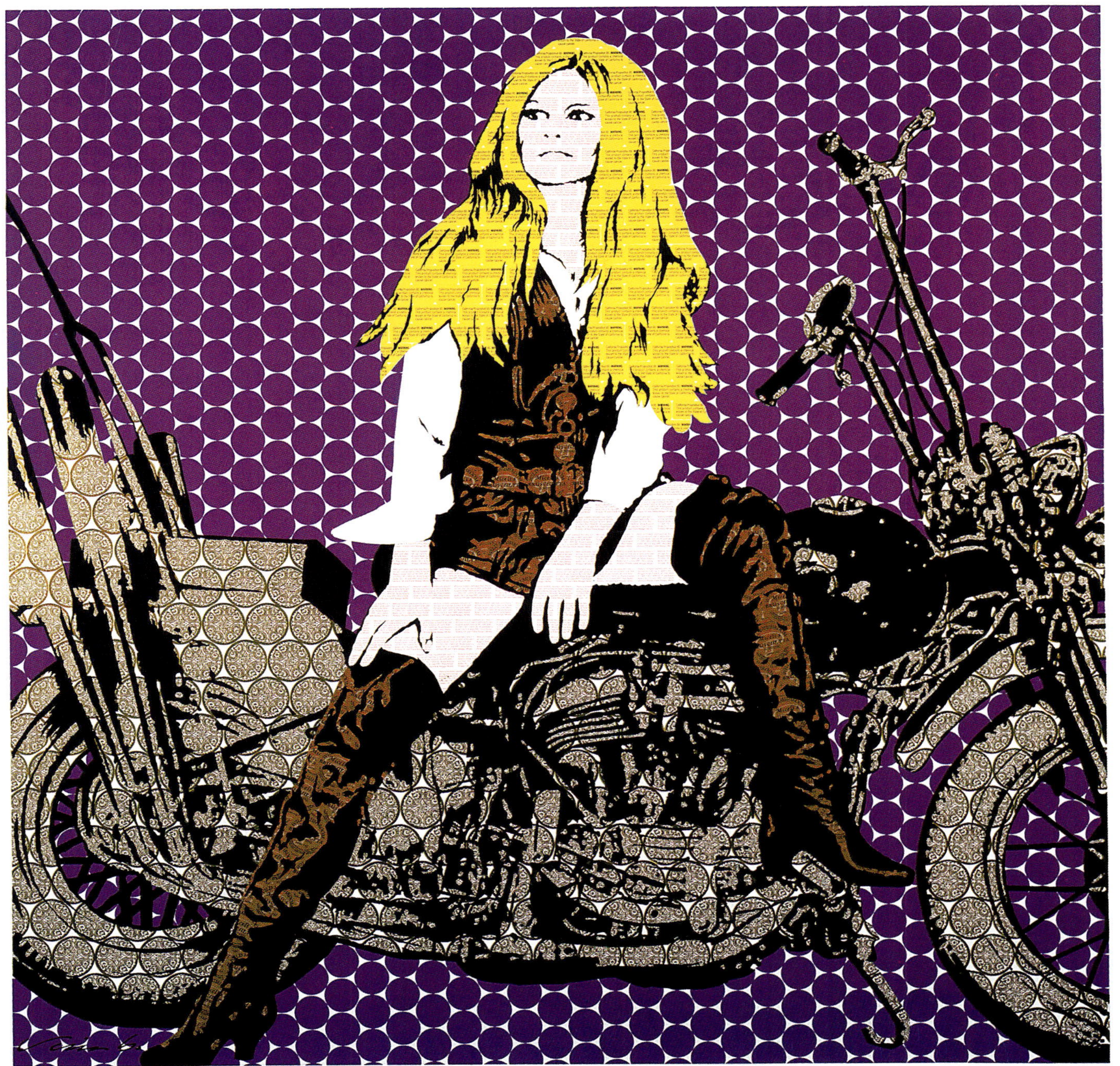

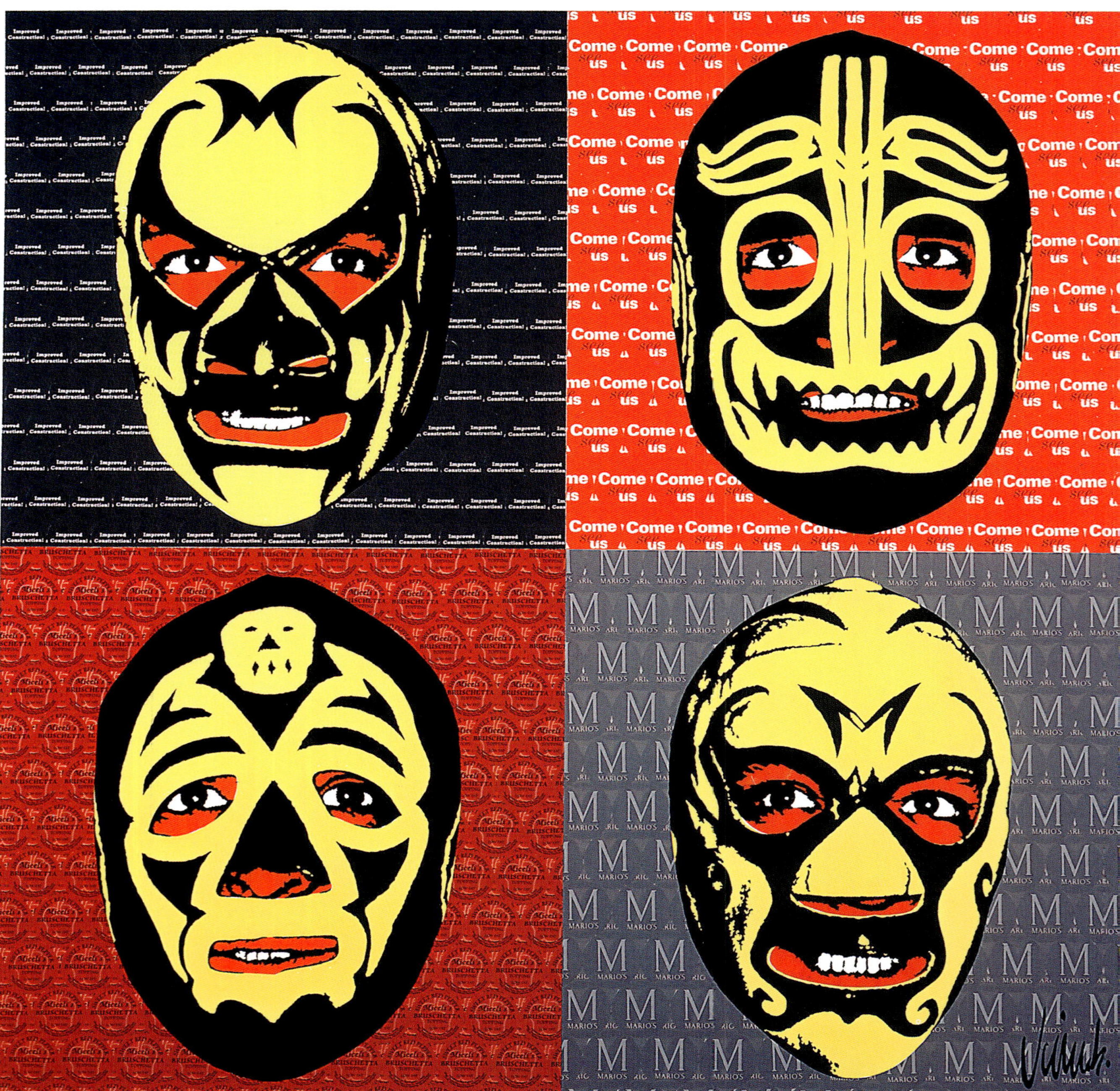

Improved Construction!
Come see us
BRUSCHETTA
M MARIO'S

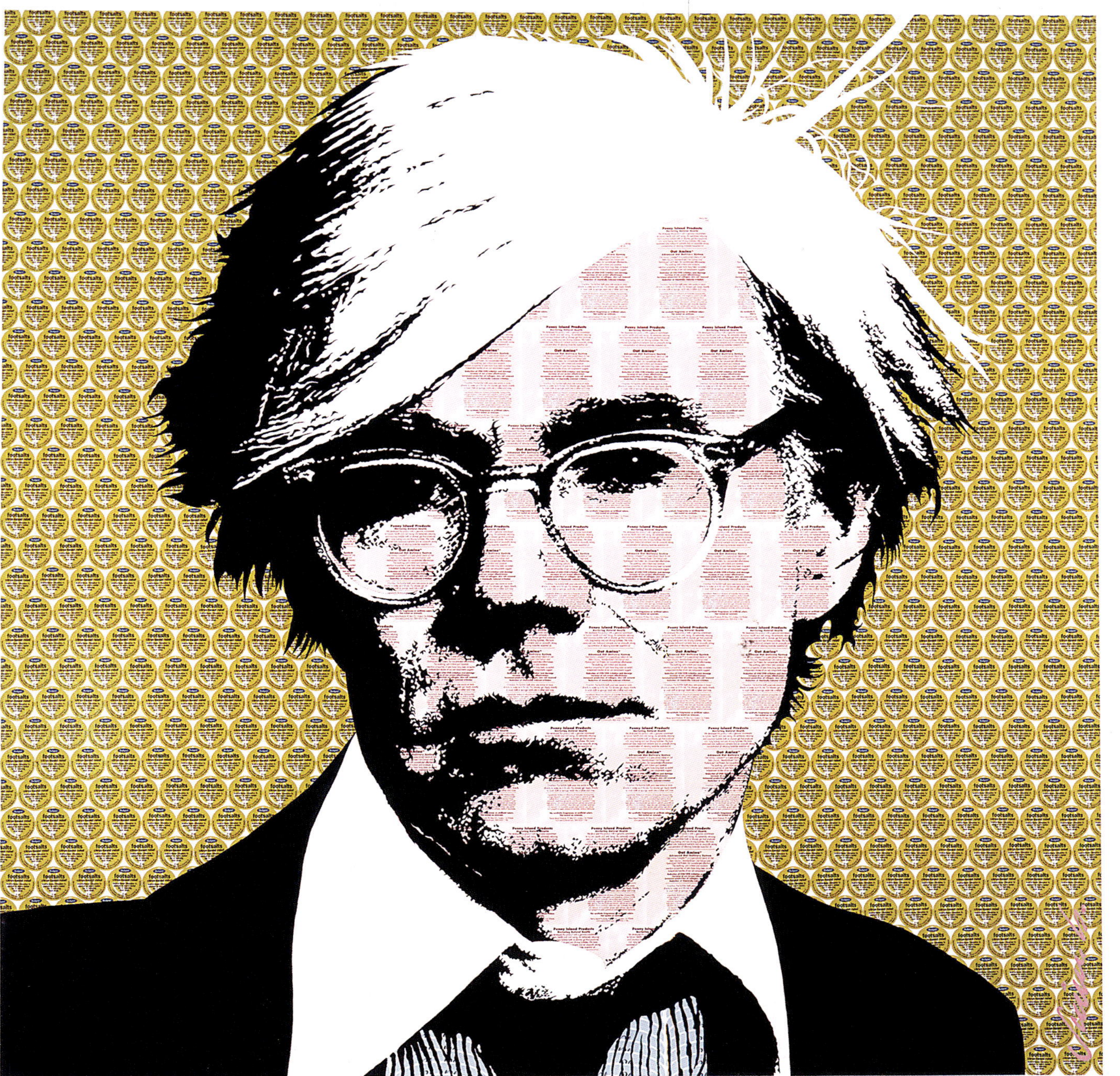
footsalts

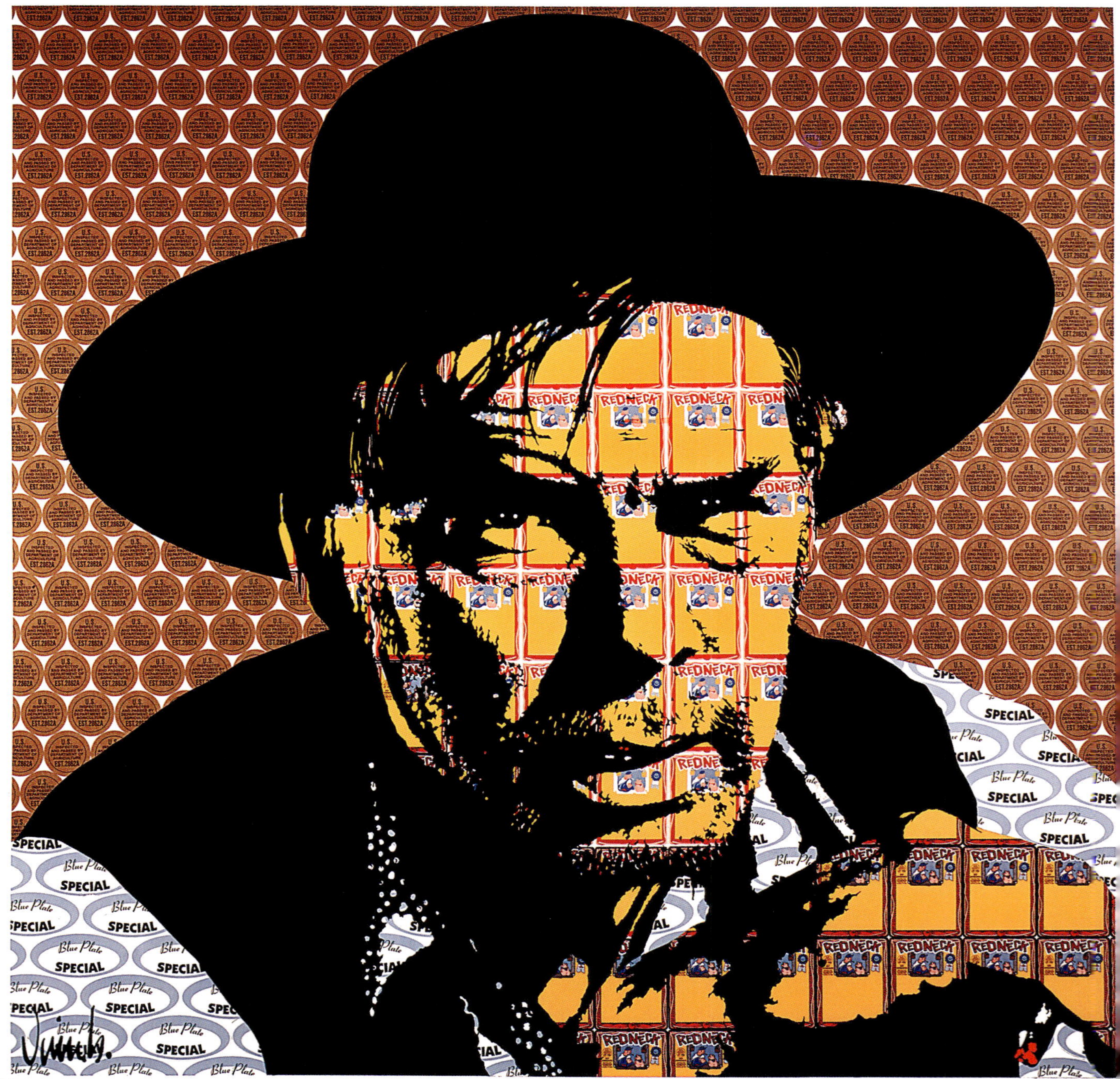
U.S.
EST.2862A
REDNECK
Blue Plate
SPECIAL

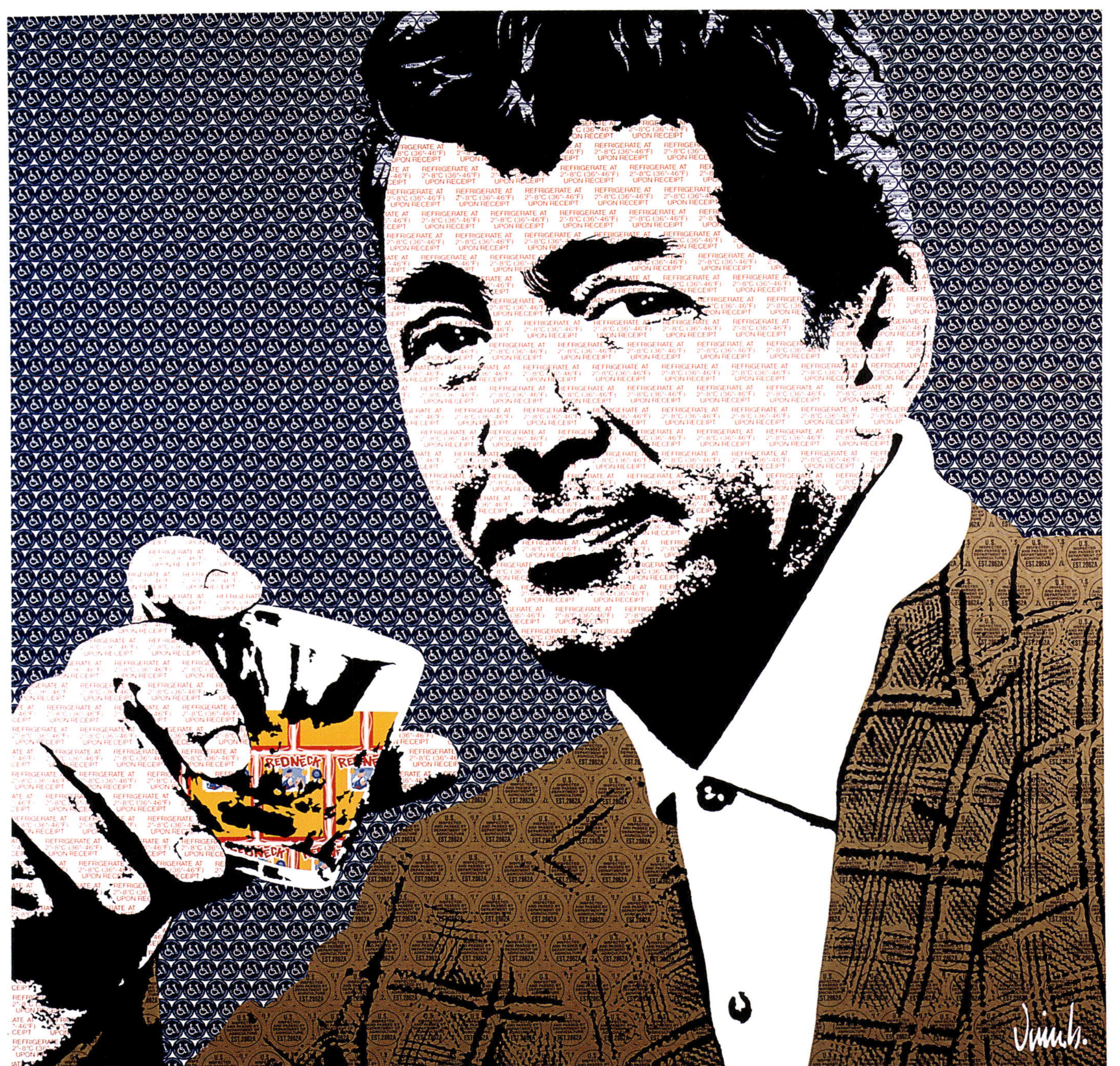
REFRIGERATE AT
2°-8°C (36°-46°F)
UPON RECEIPT
REDNECK
EST.2862A

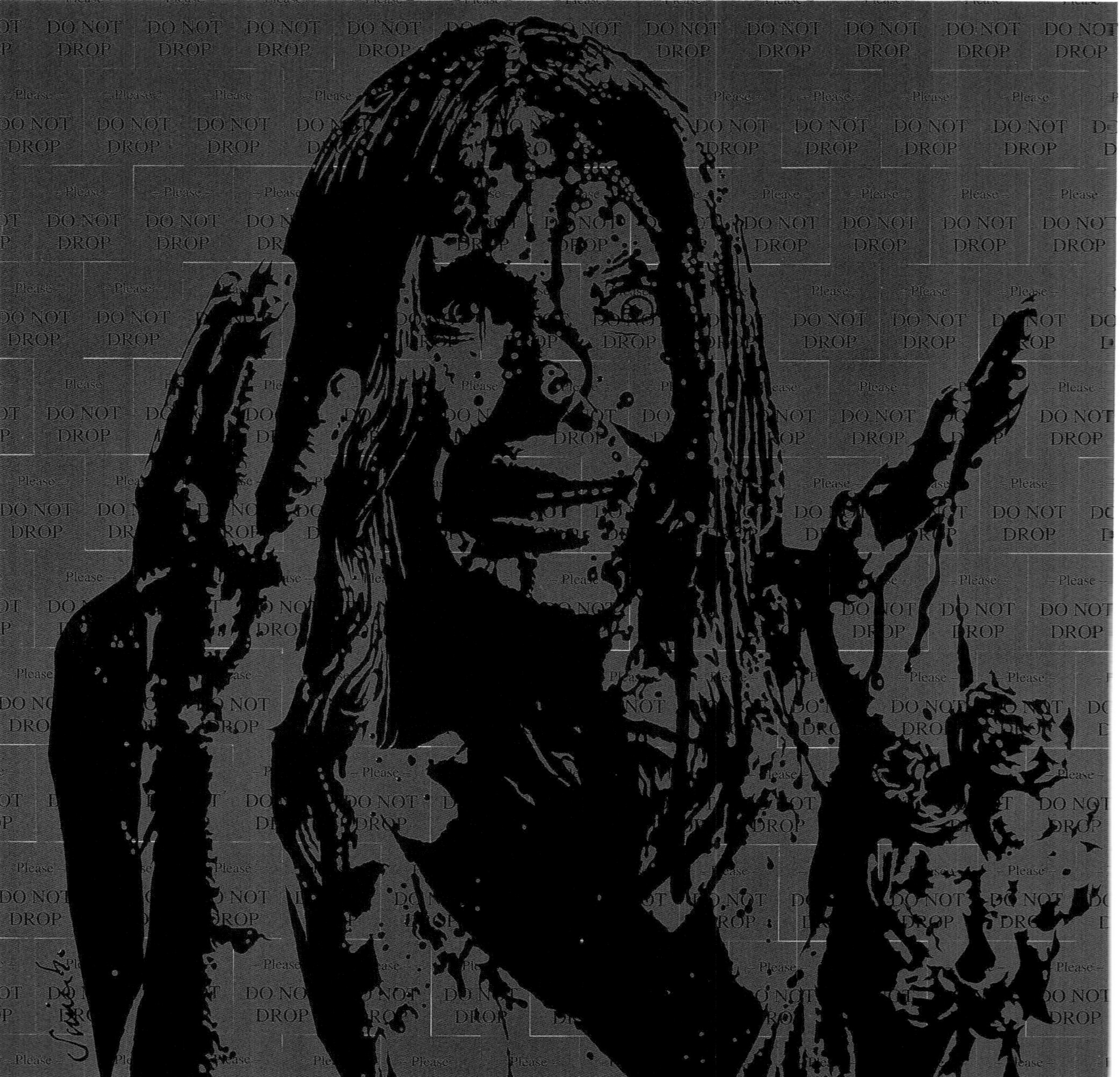
– Please –
DO NOT
DROP

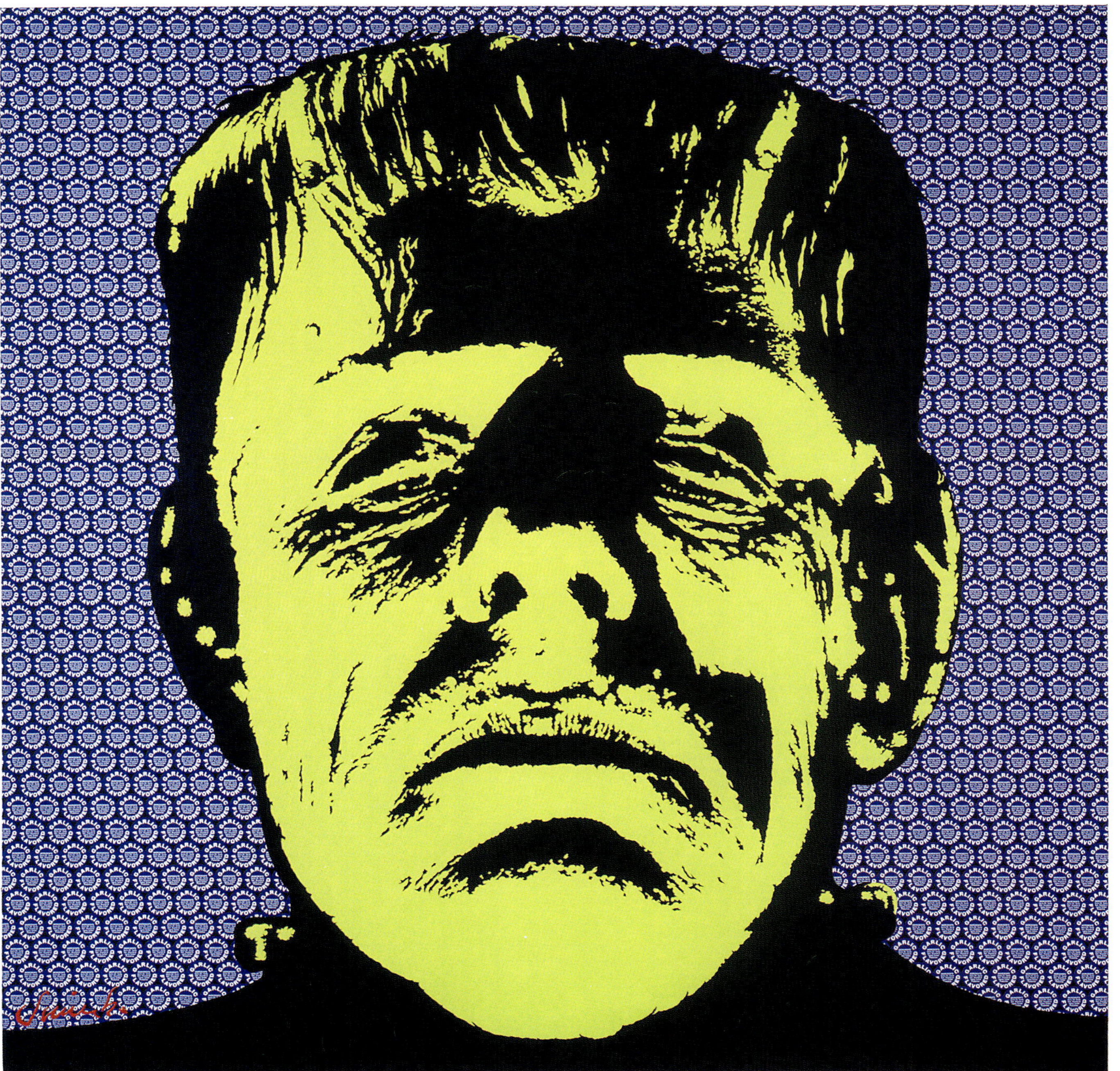

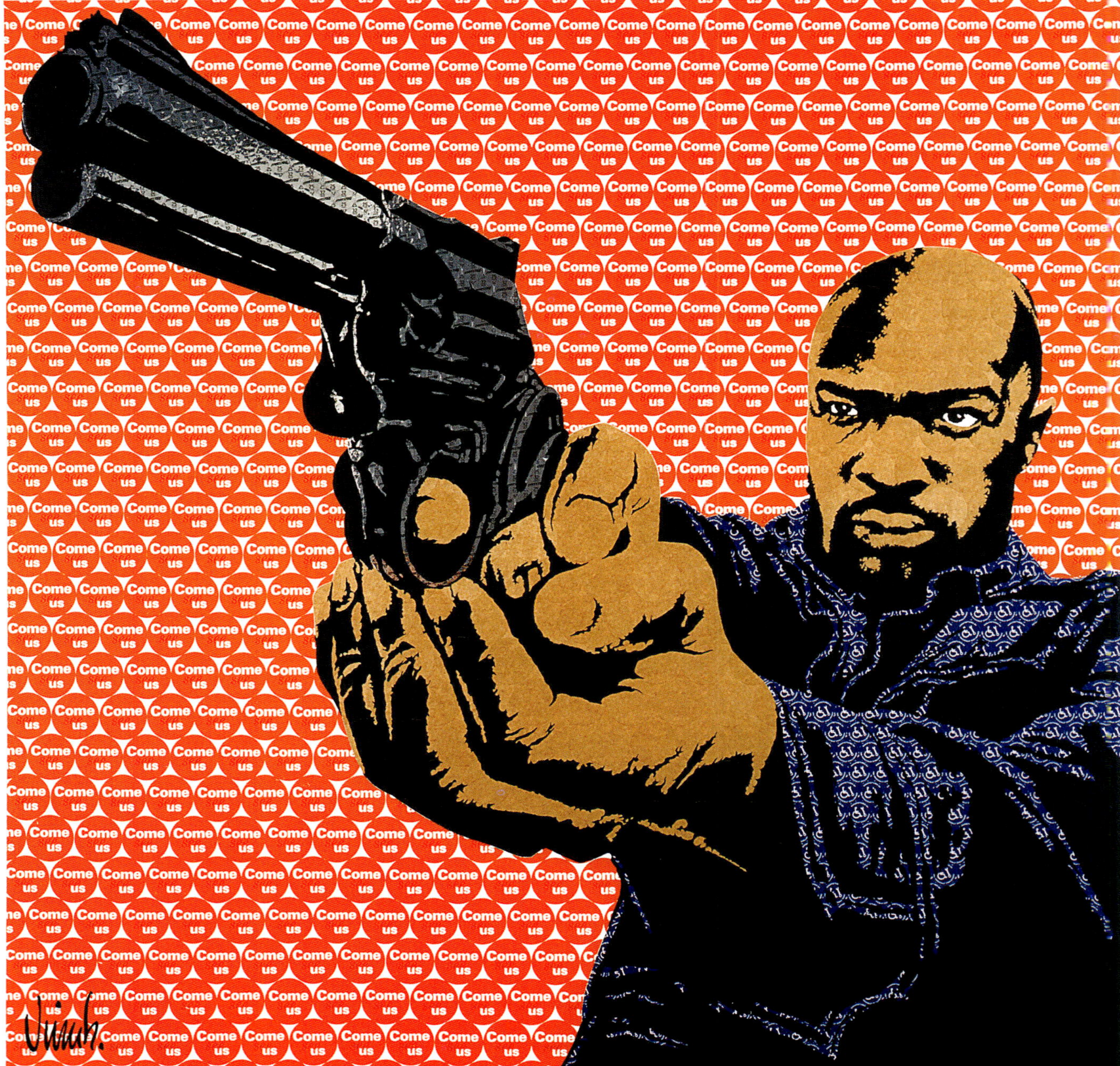
Come
us

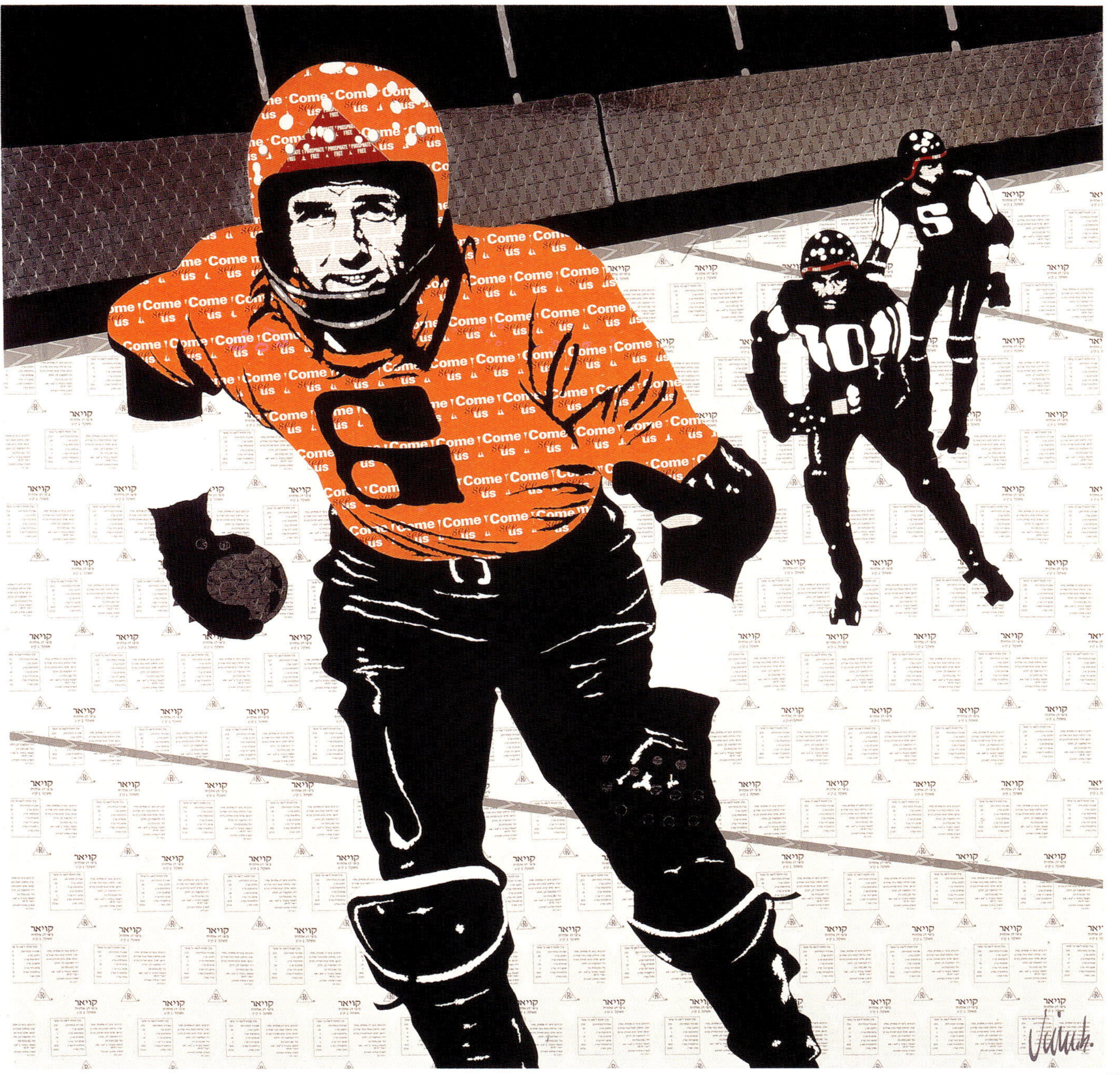
Come see us
קויאר

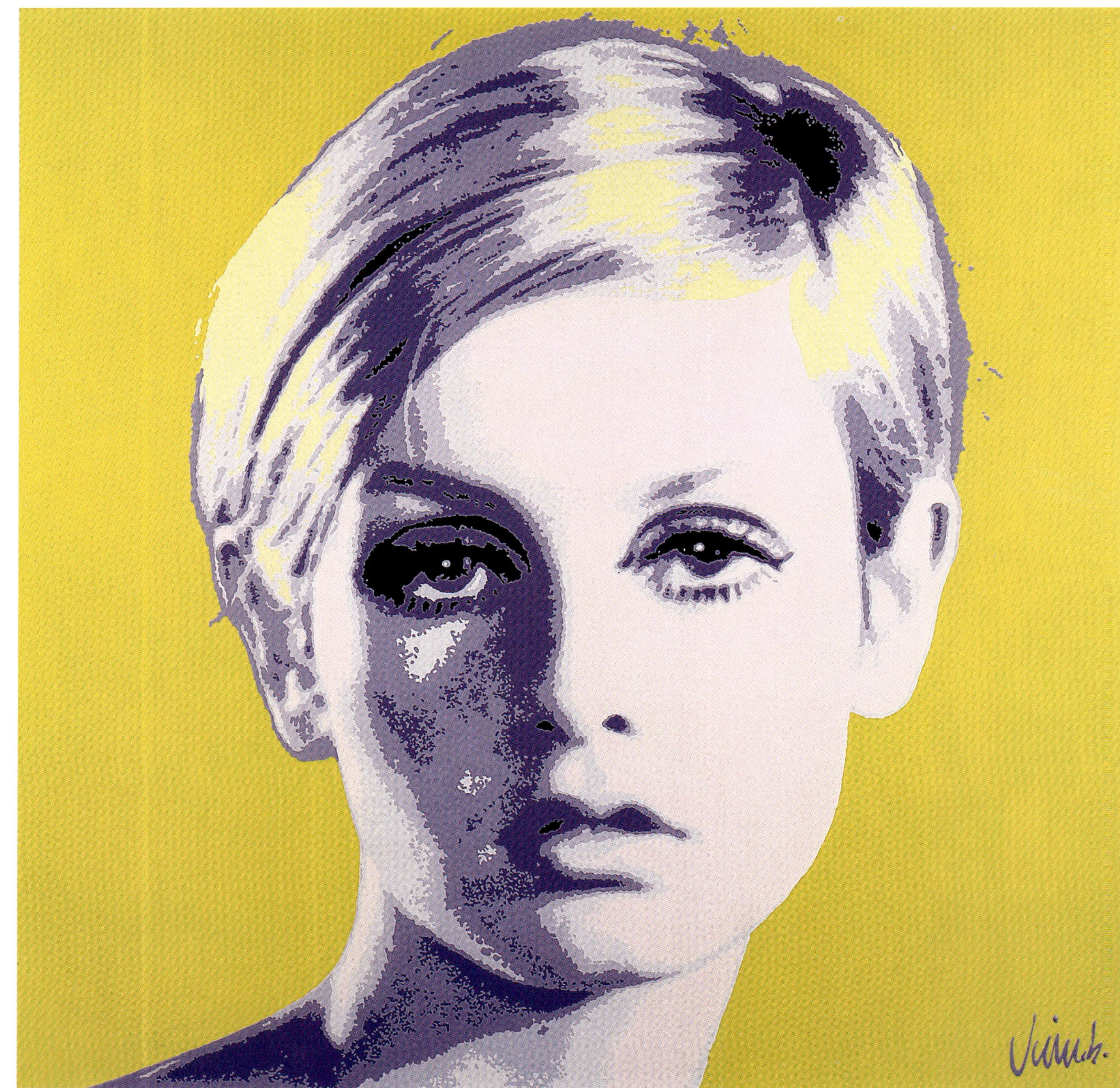

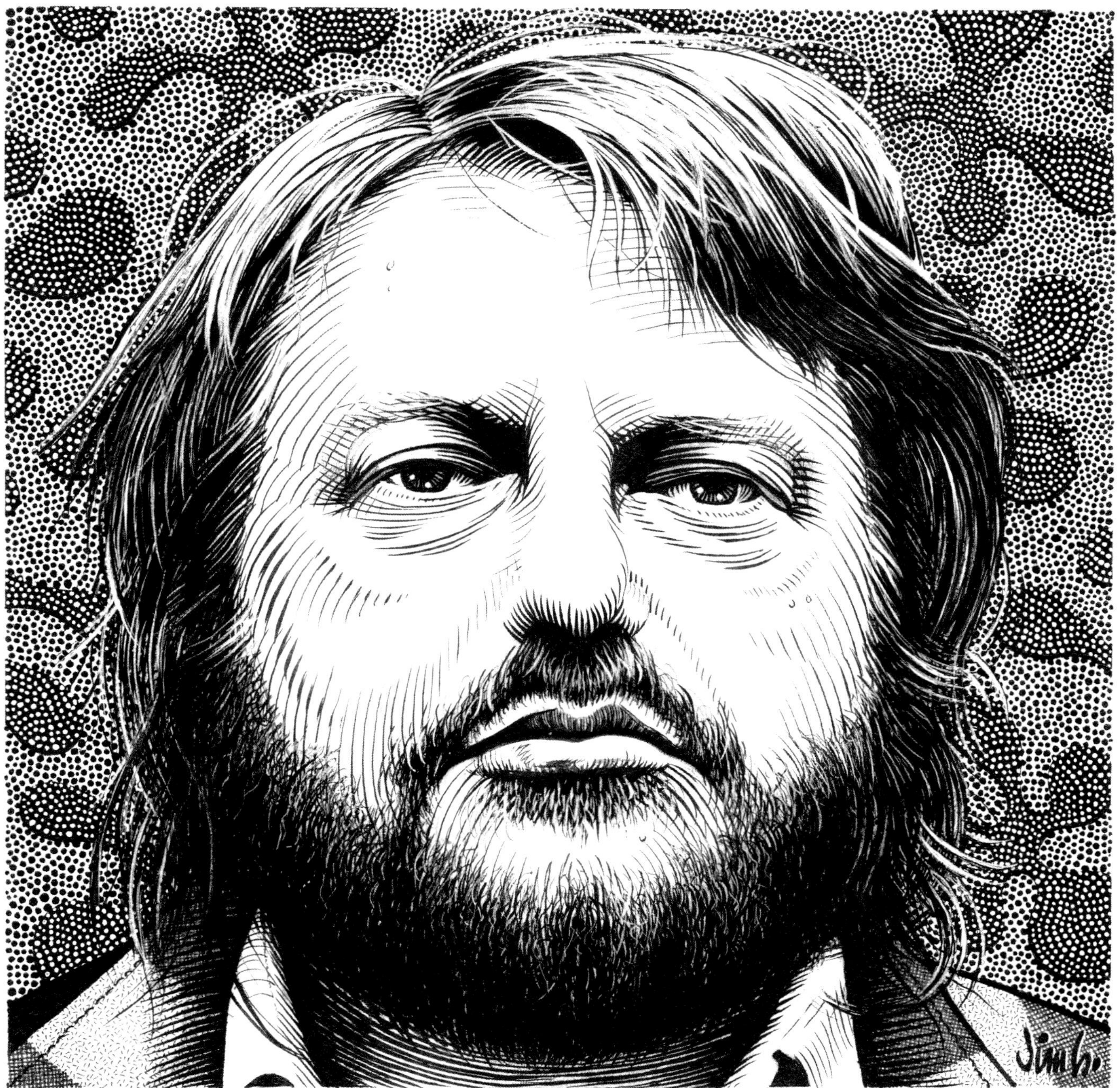
Jim W.

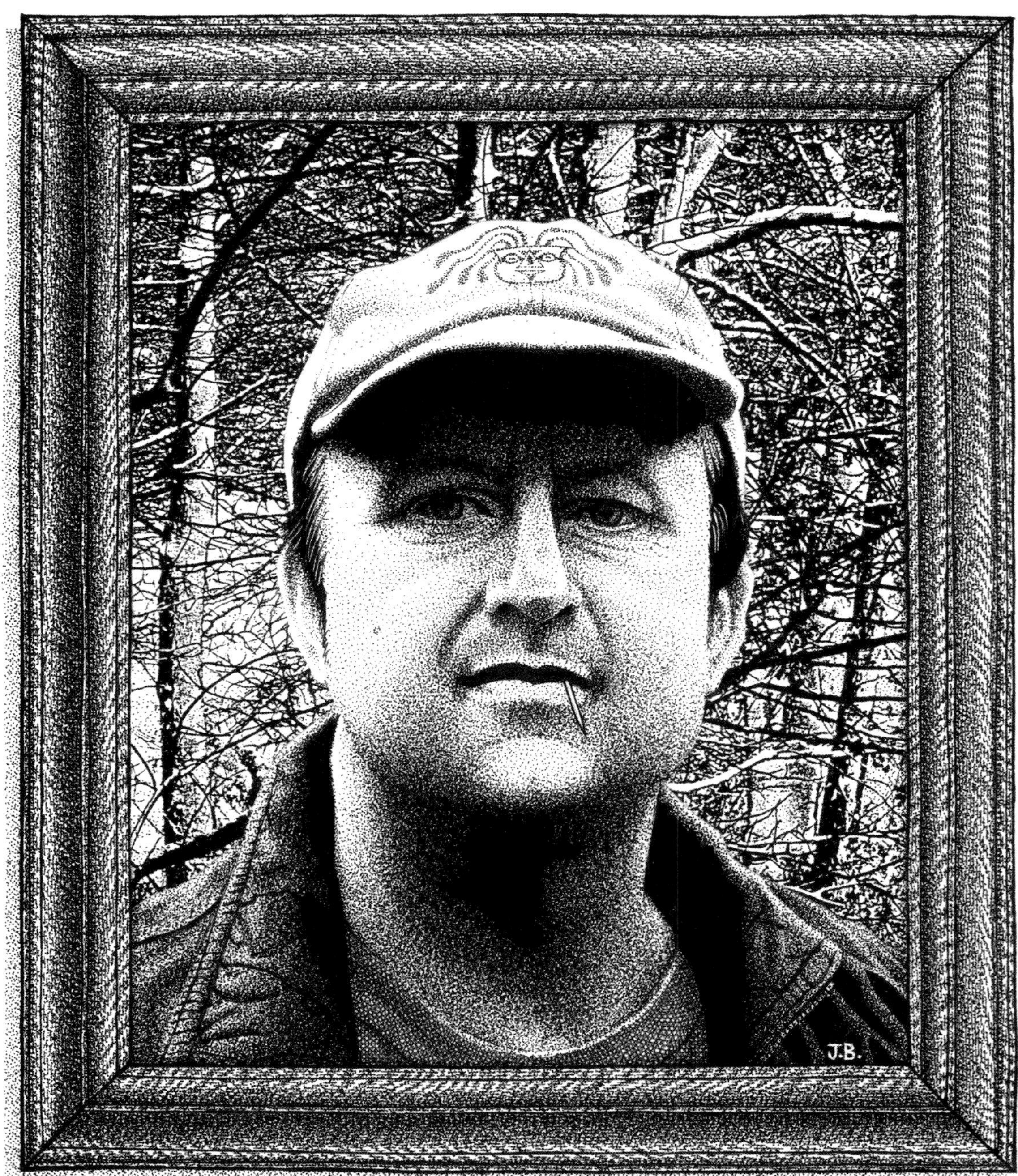
J.B.

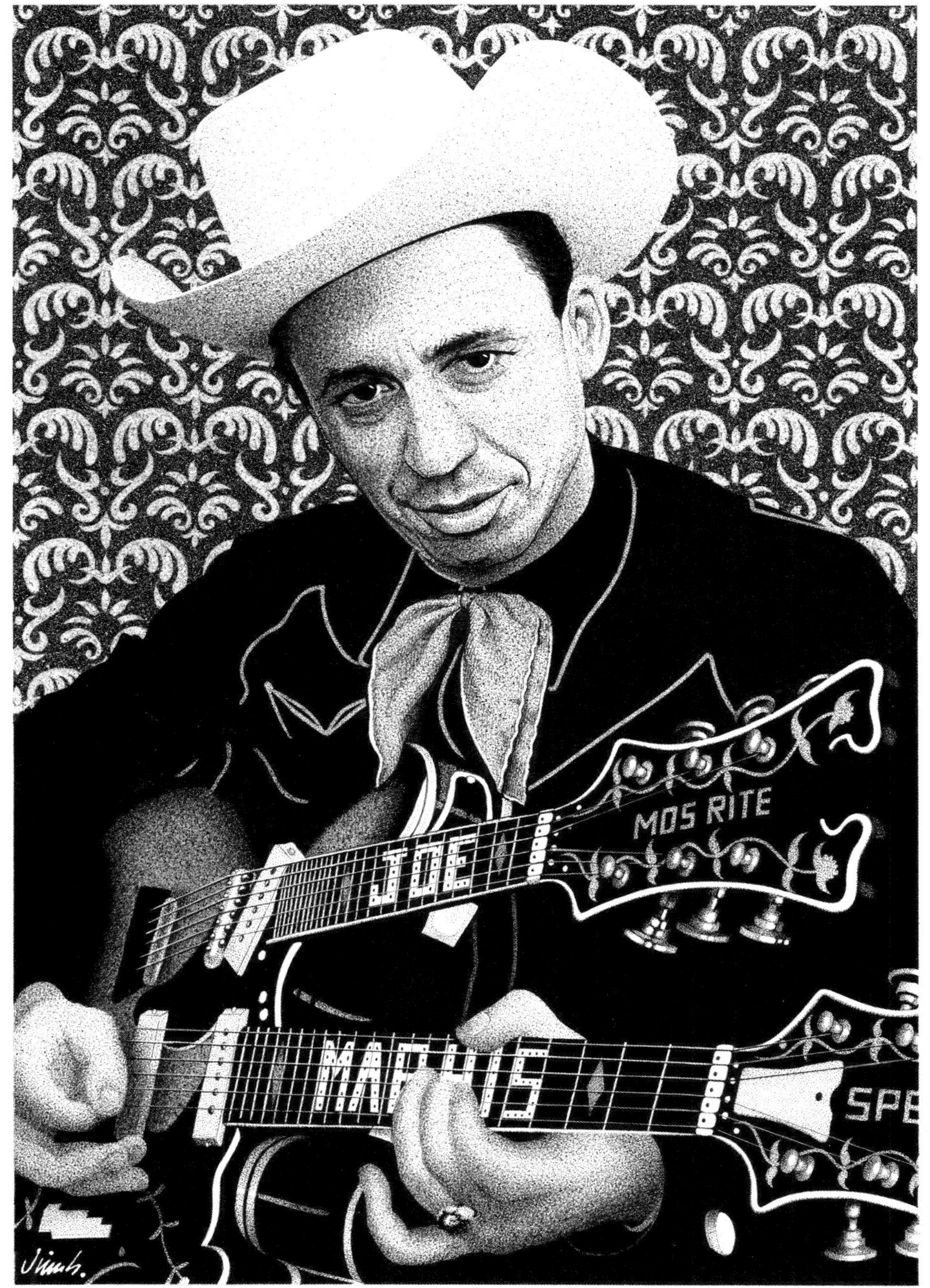
MOS RITE
JOE
MAPHIS

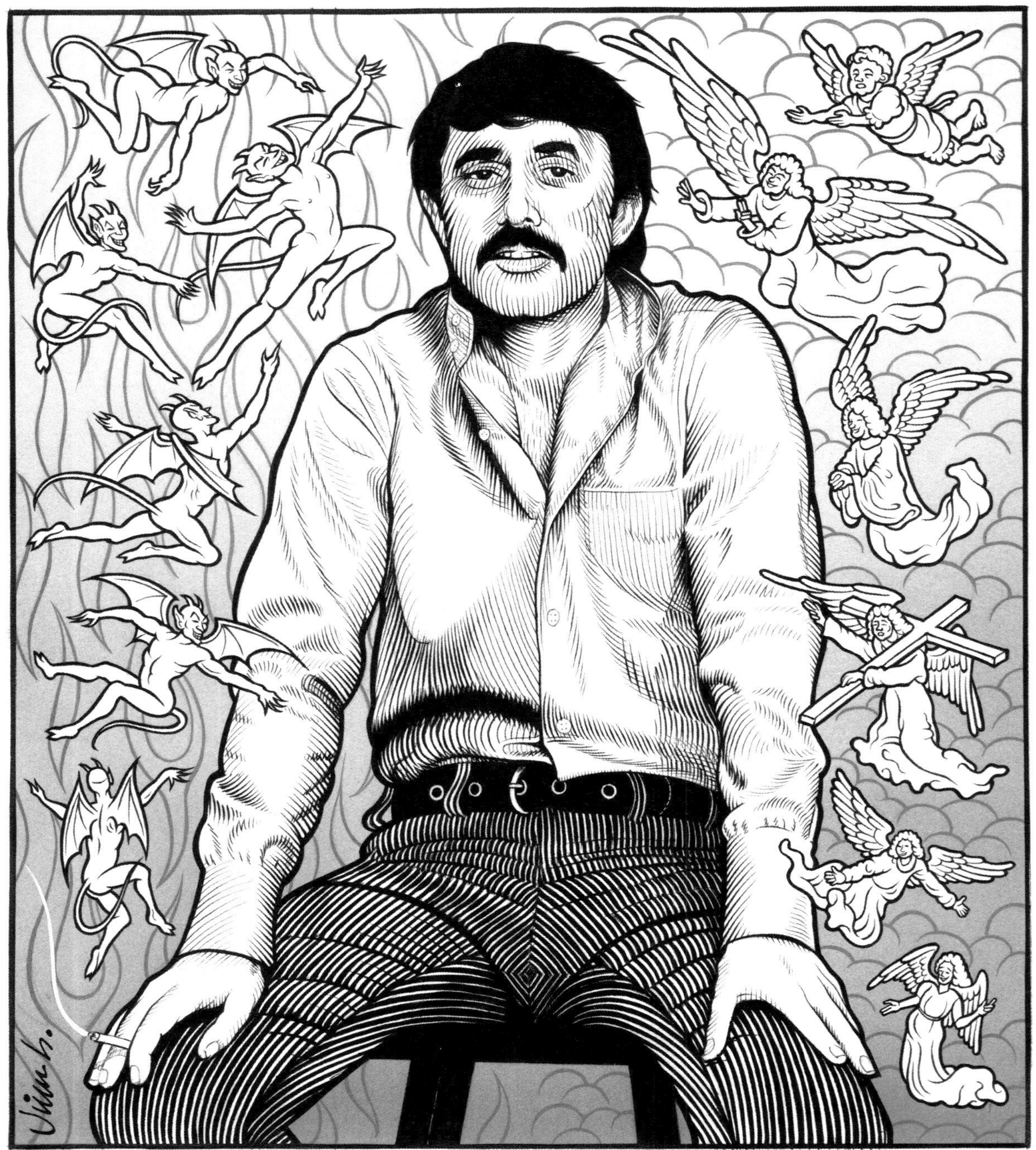

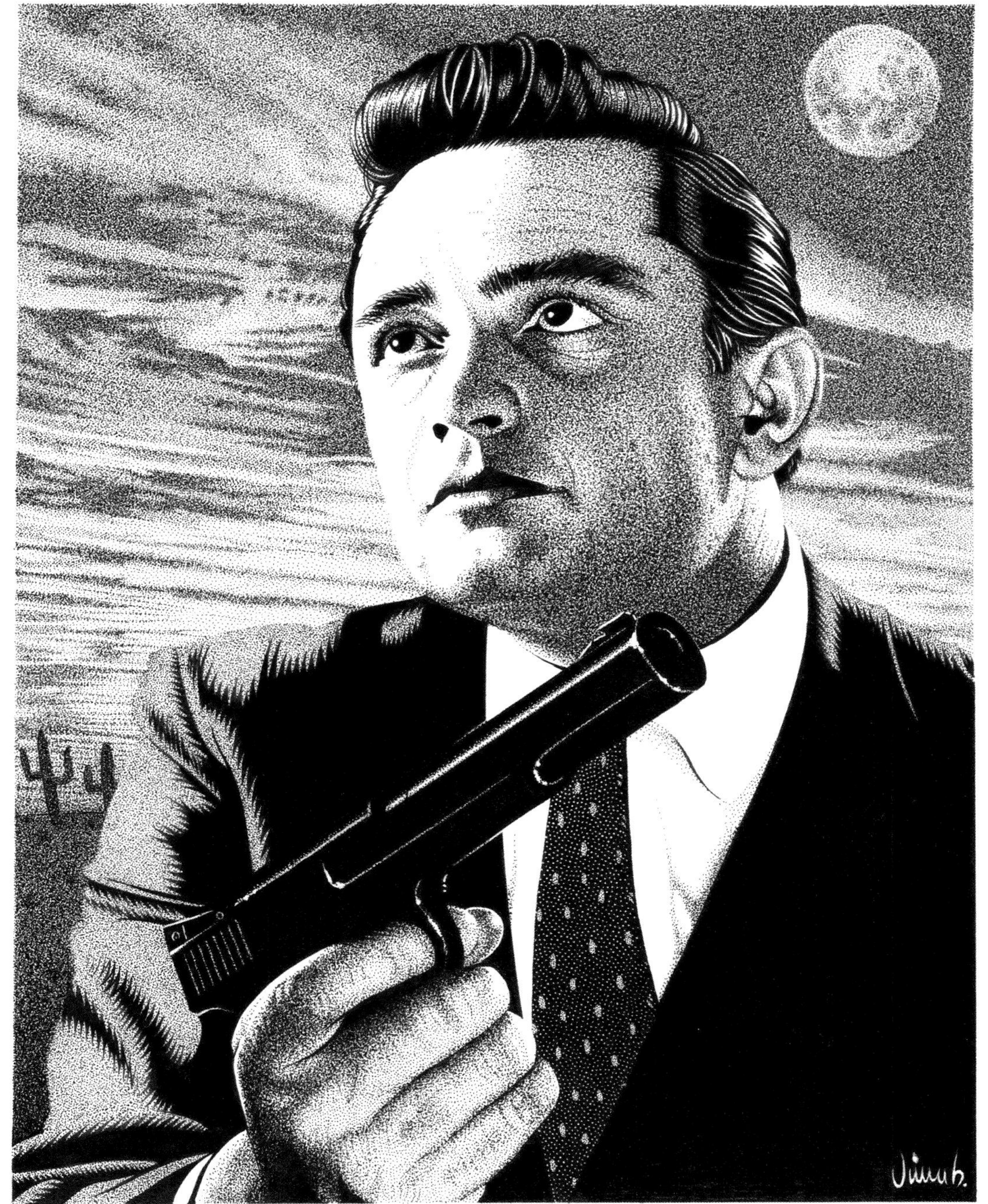

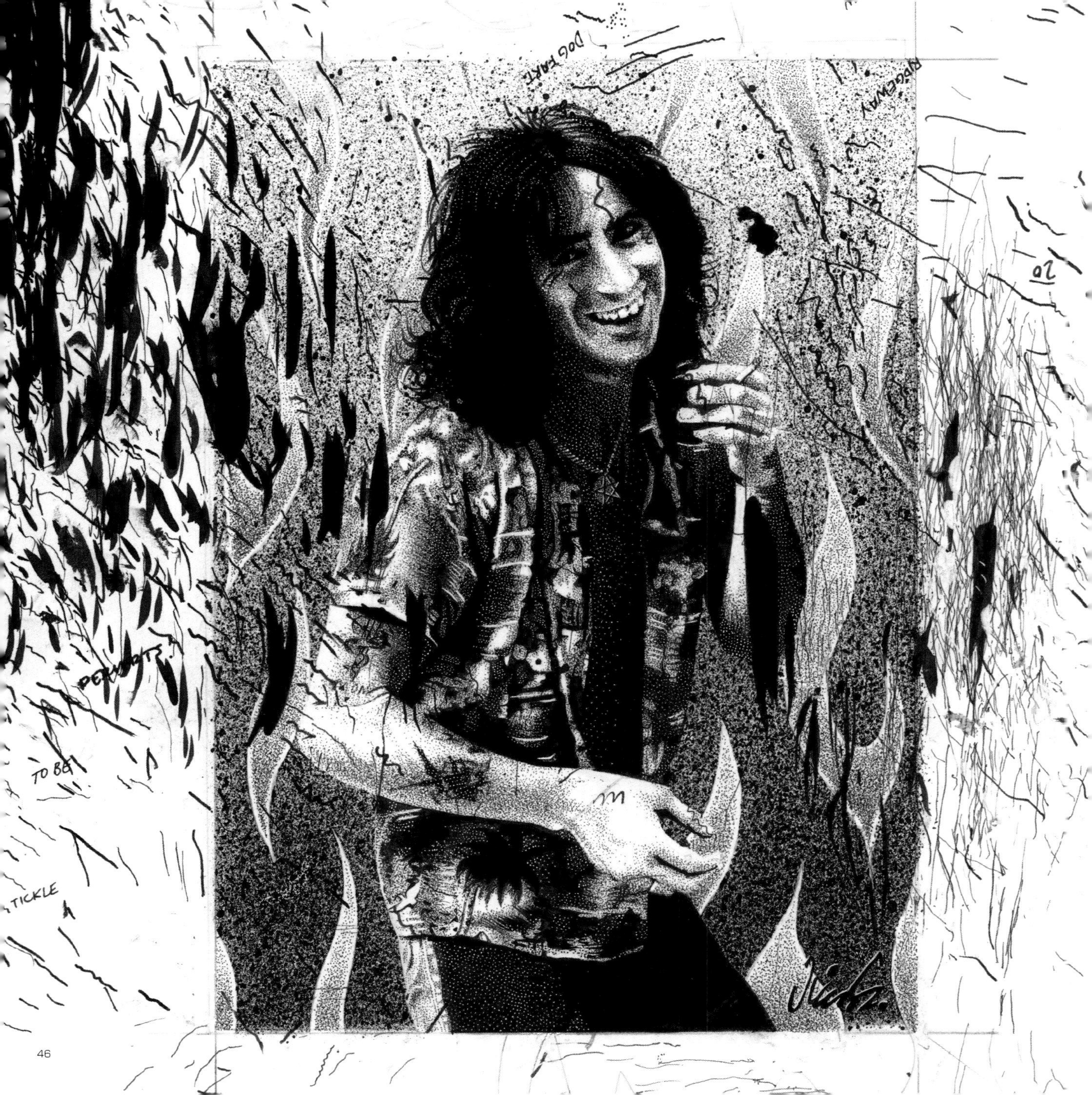
02
TO BE
TICKLE

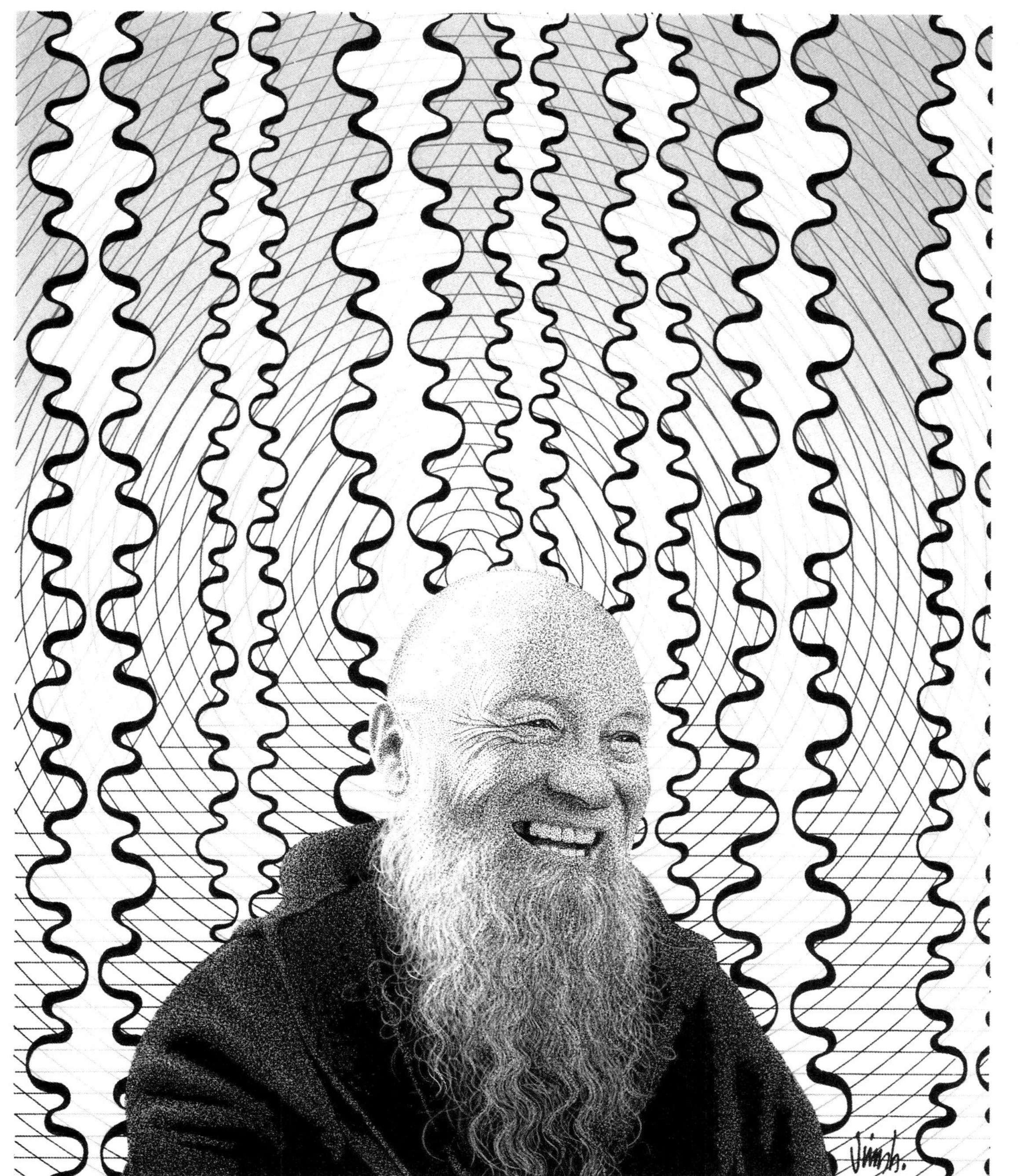

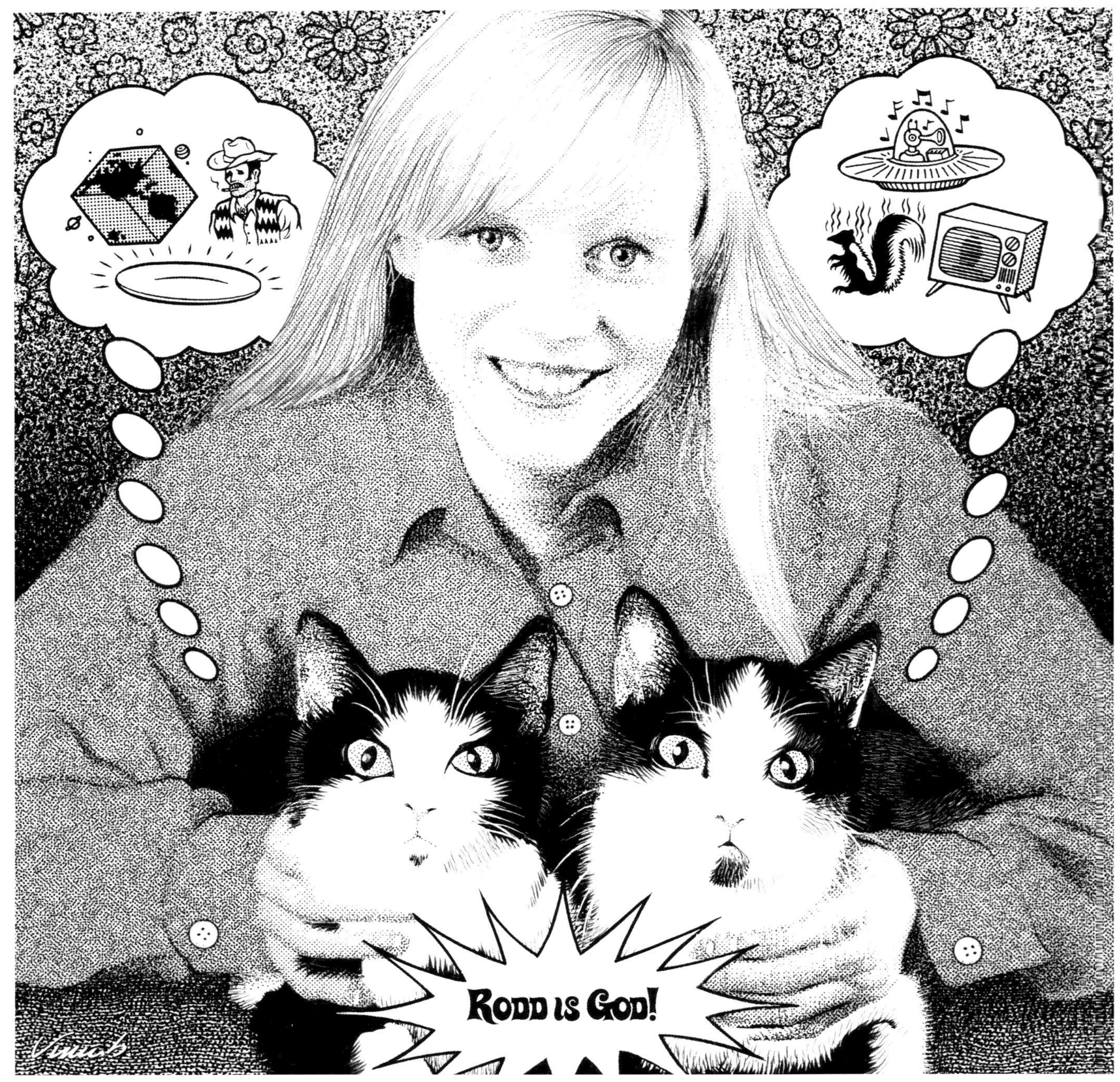
RODD IS GOD!
Vinick

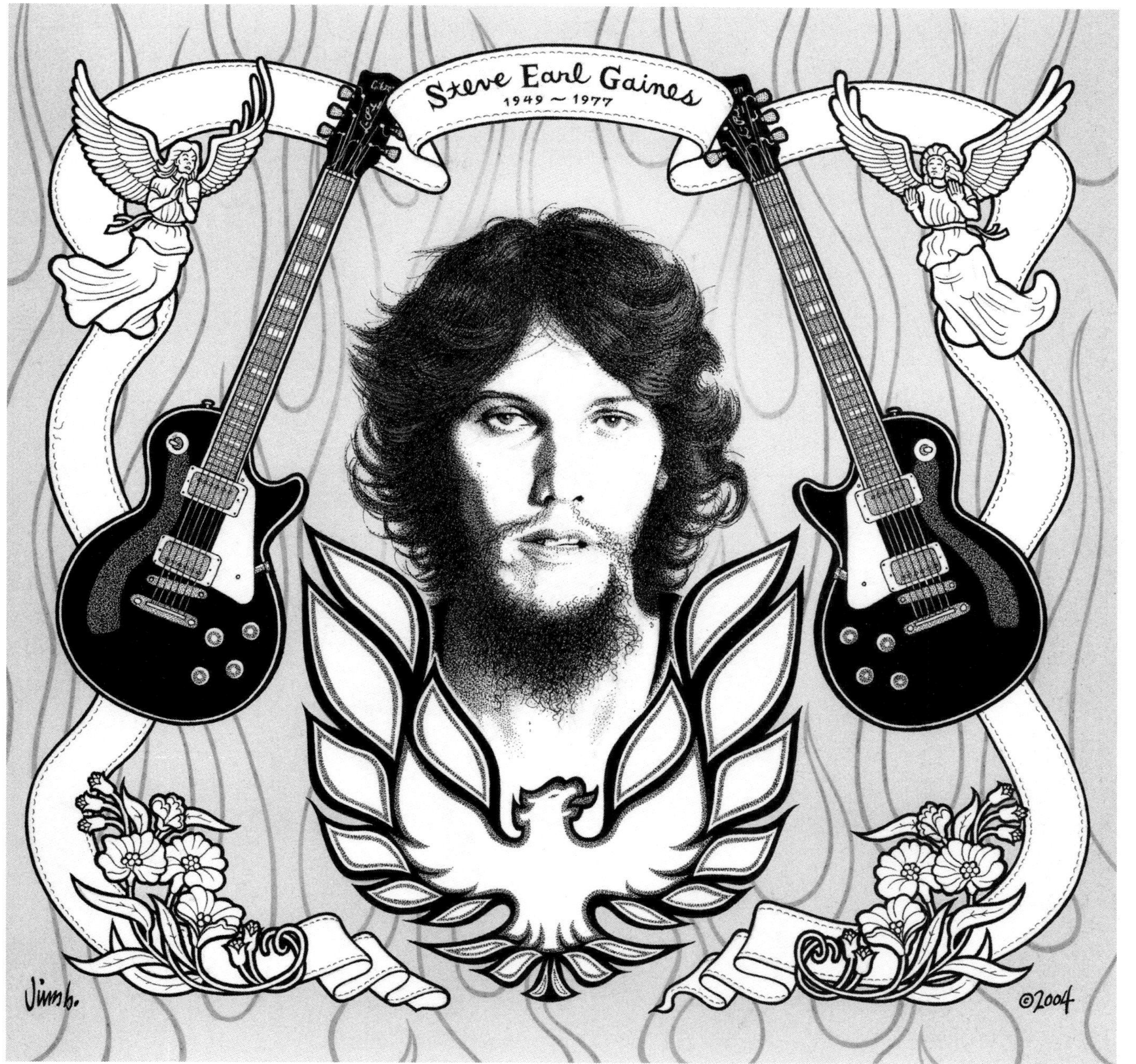
Steve Earl Gaines
1949 ~ 1977
Jim b.
©2004

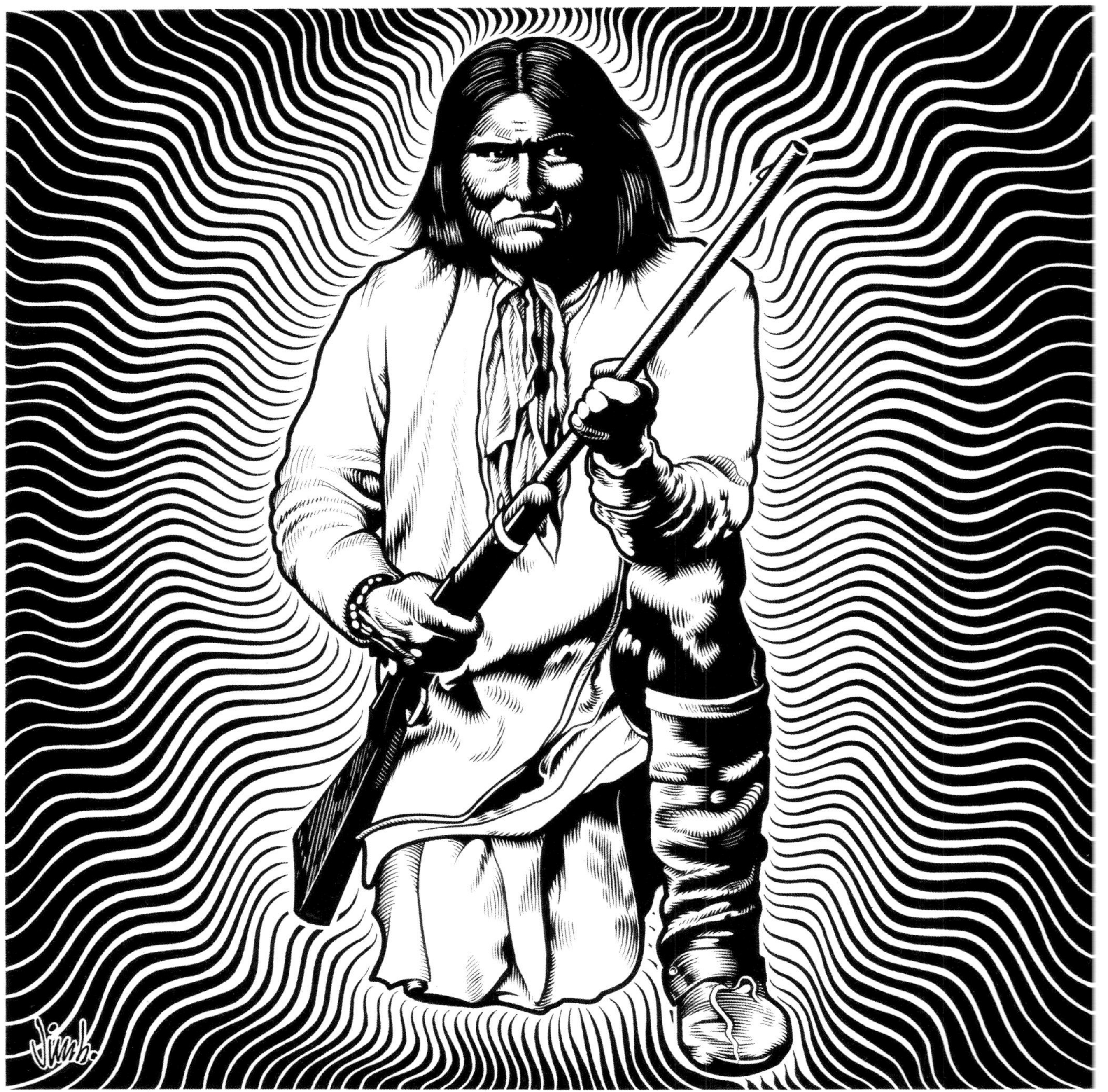

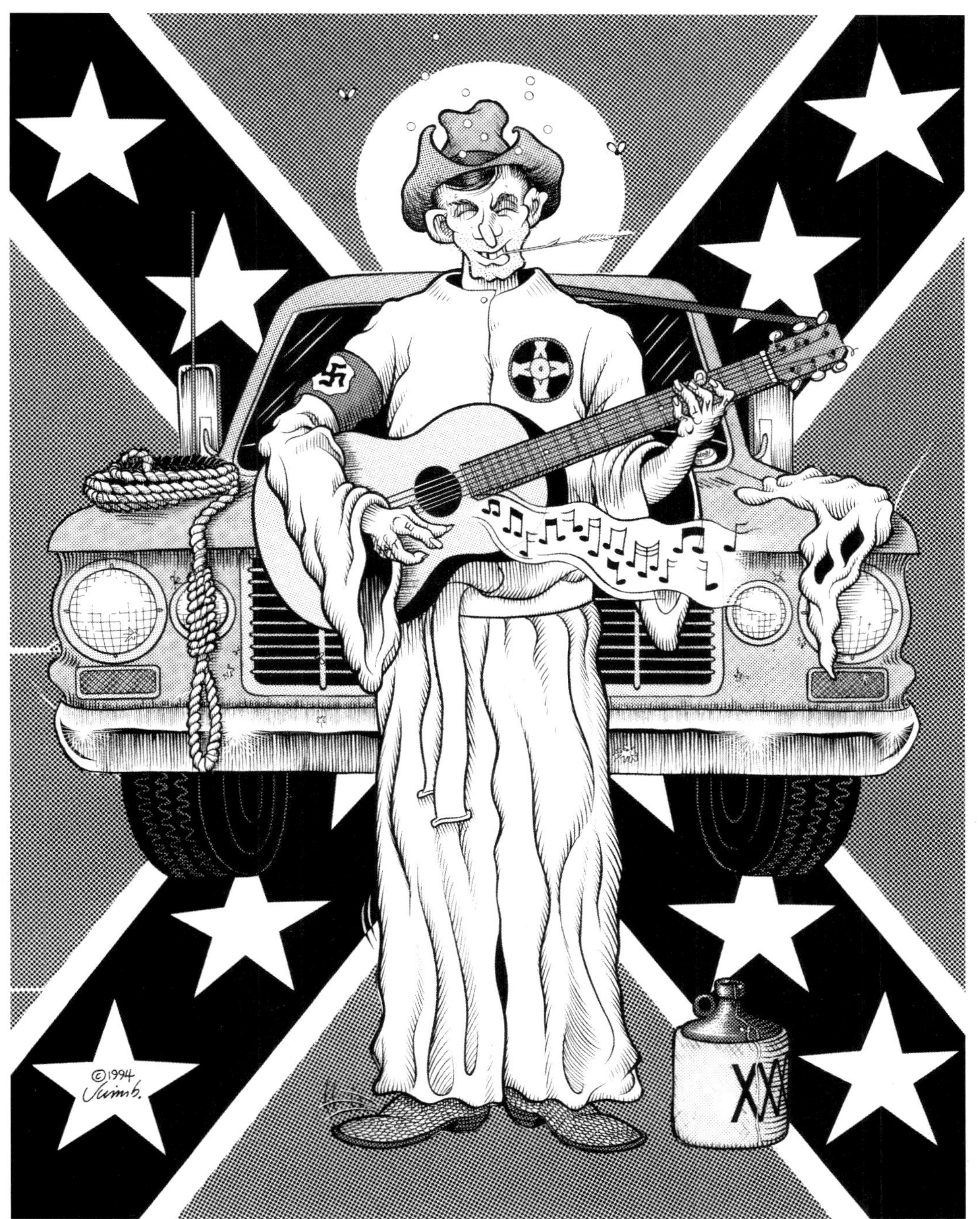
©1994
Crumb.

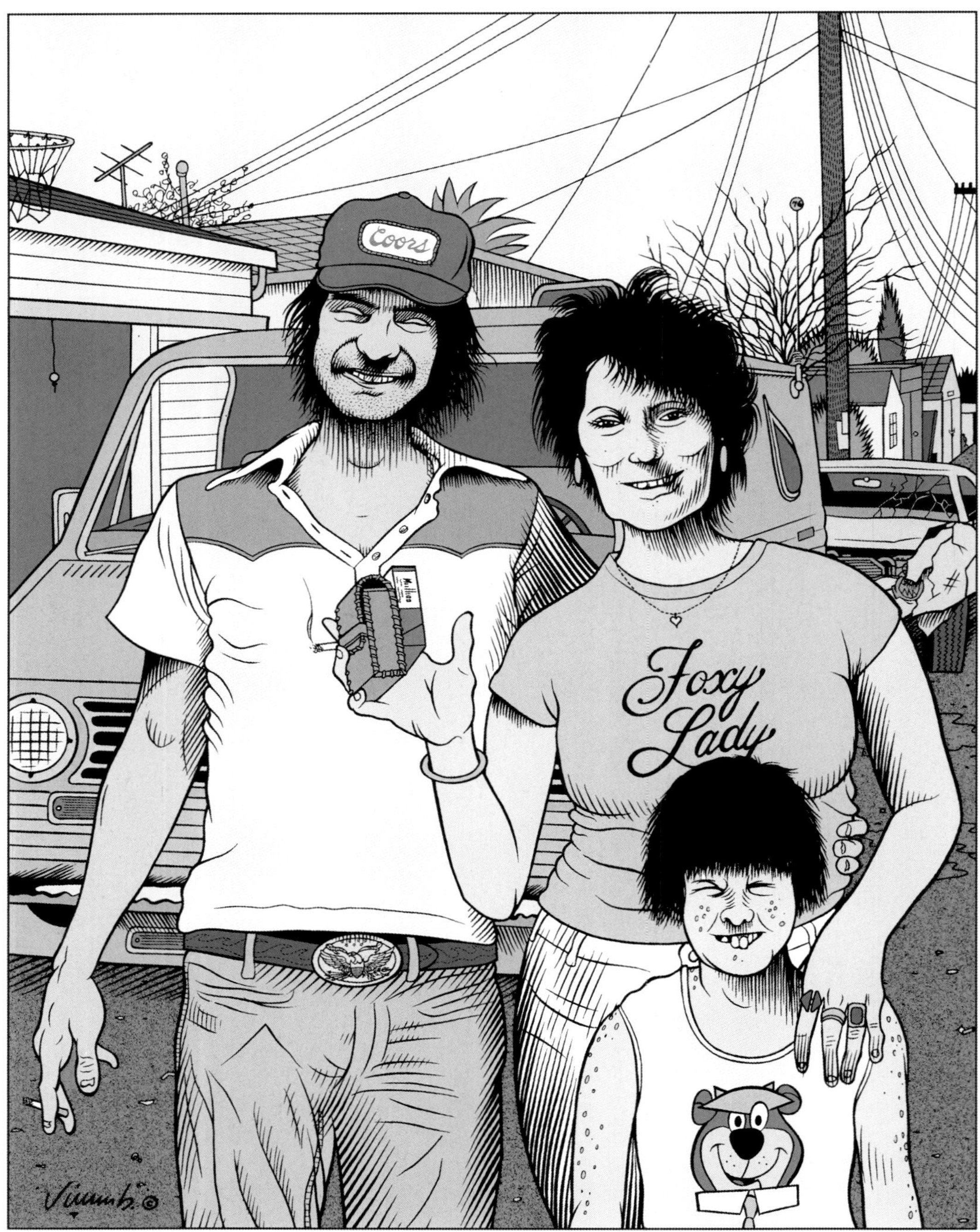
Coors
Foxy Lady

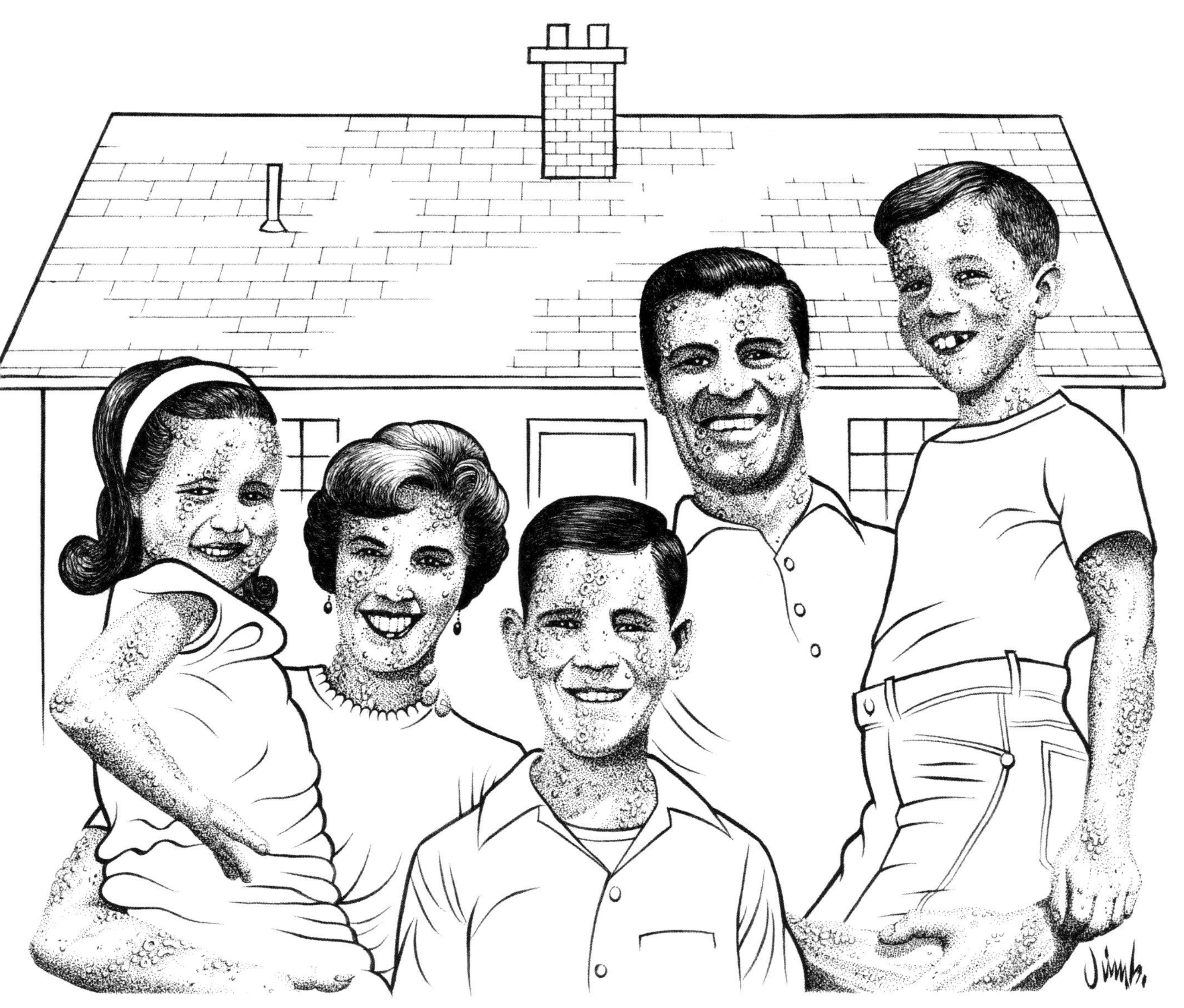

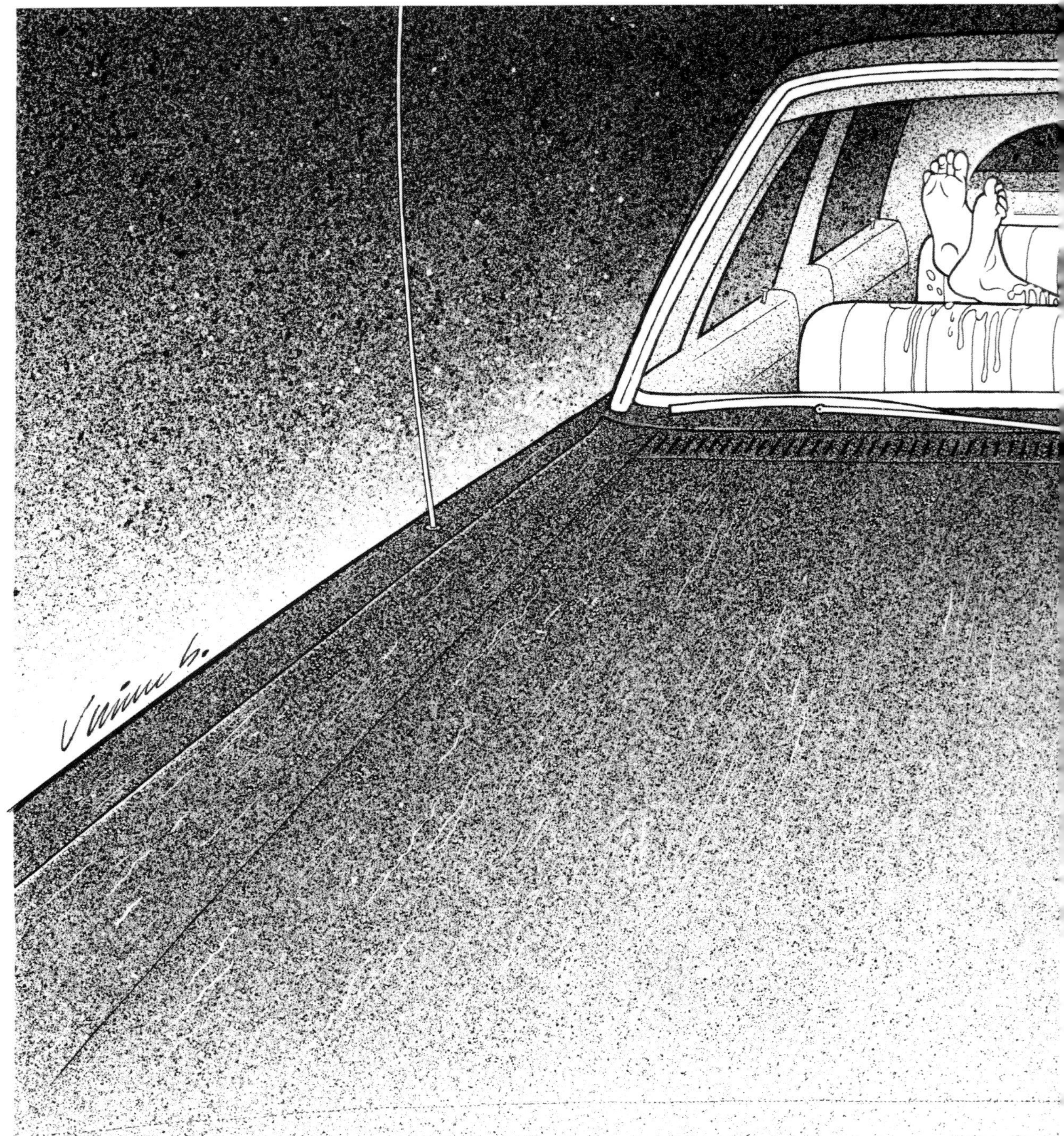

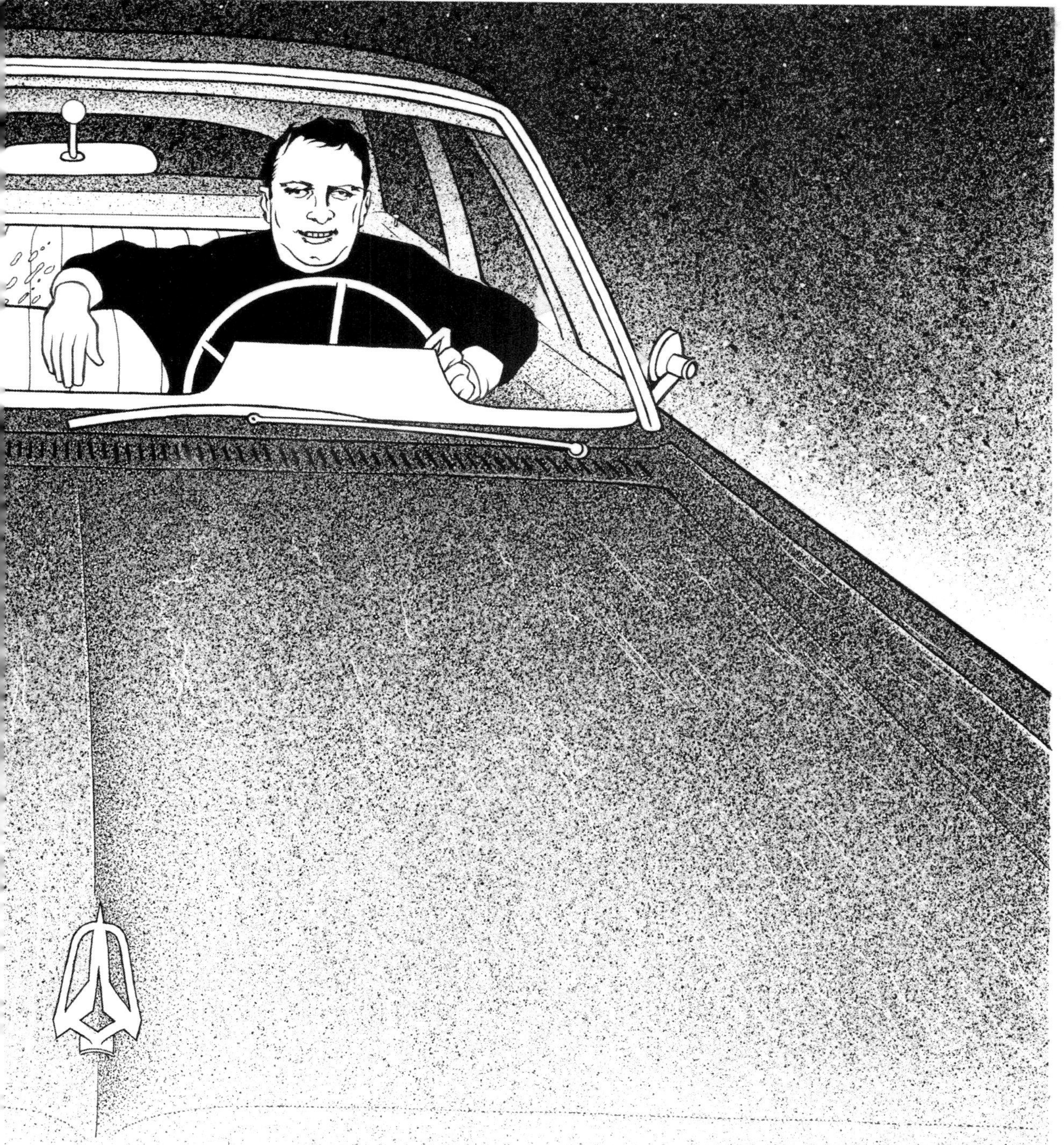

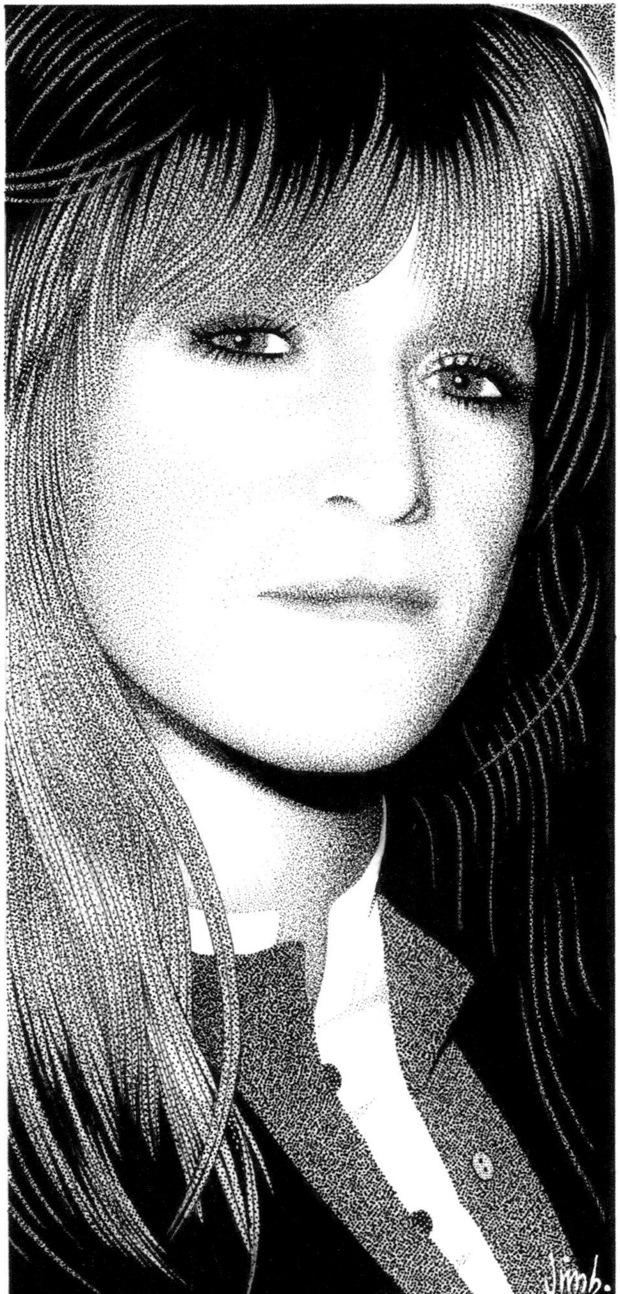

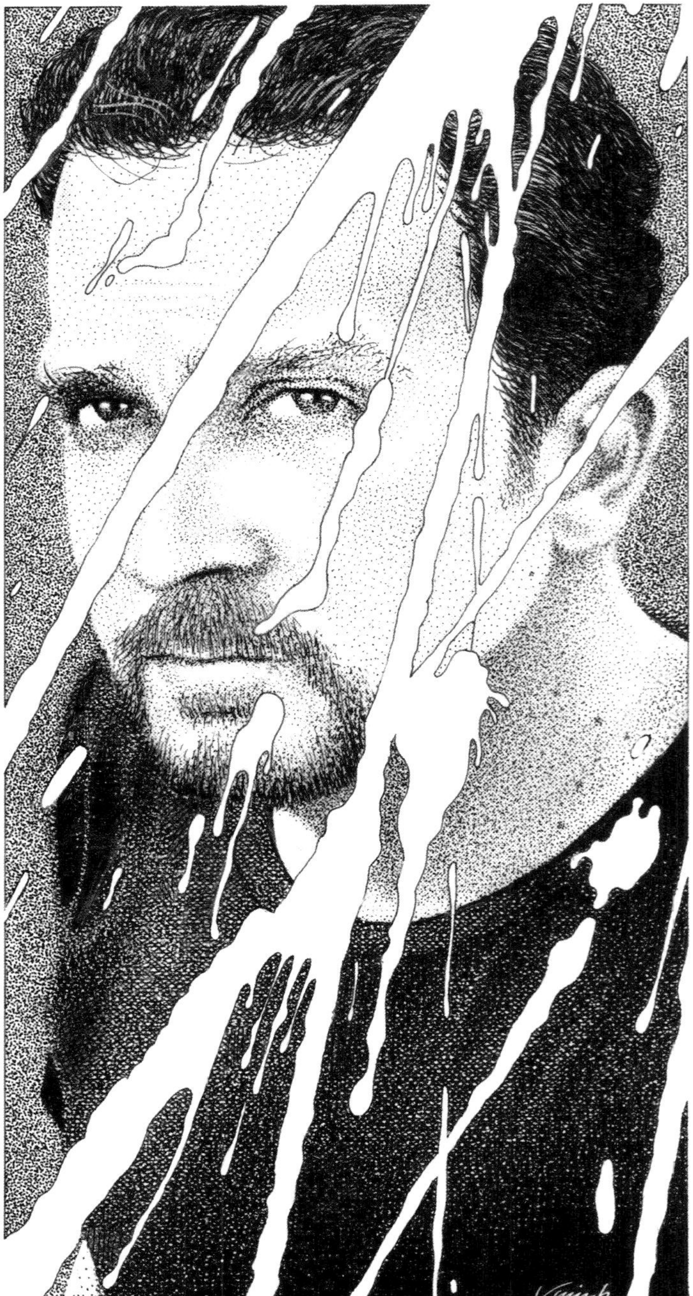

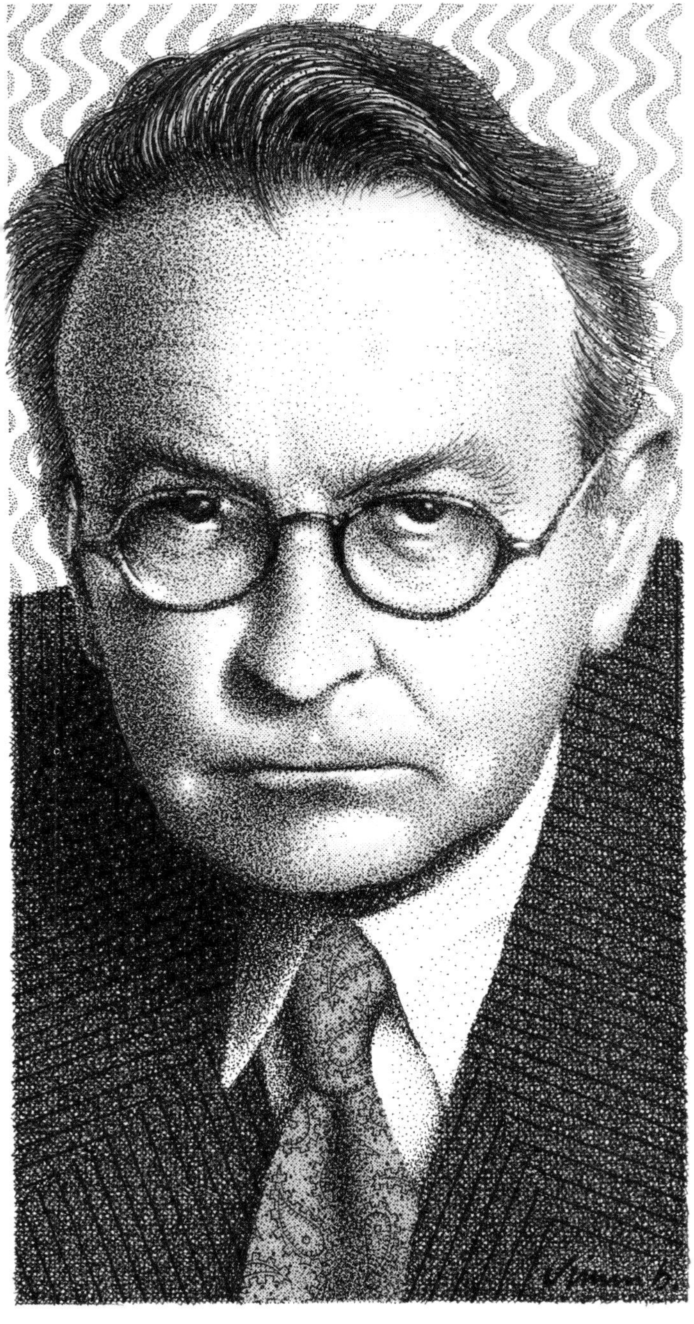

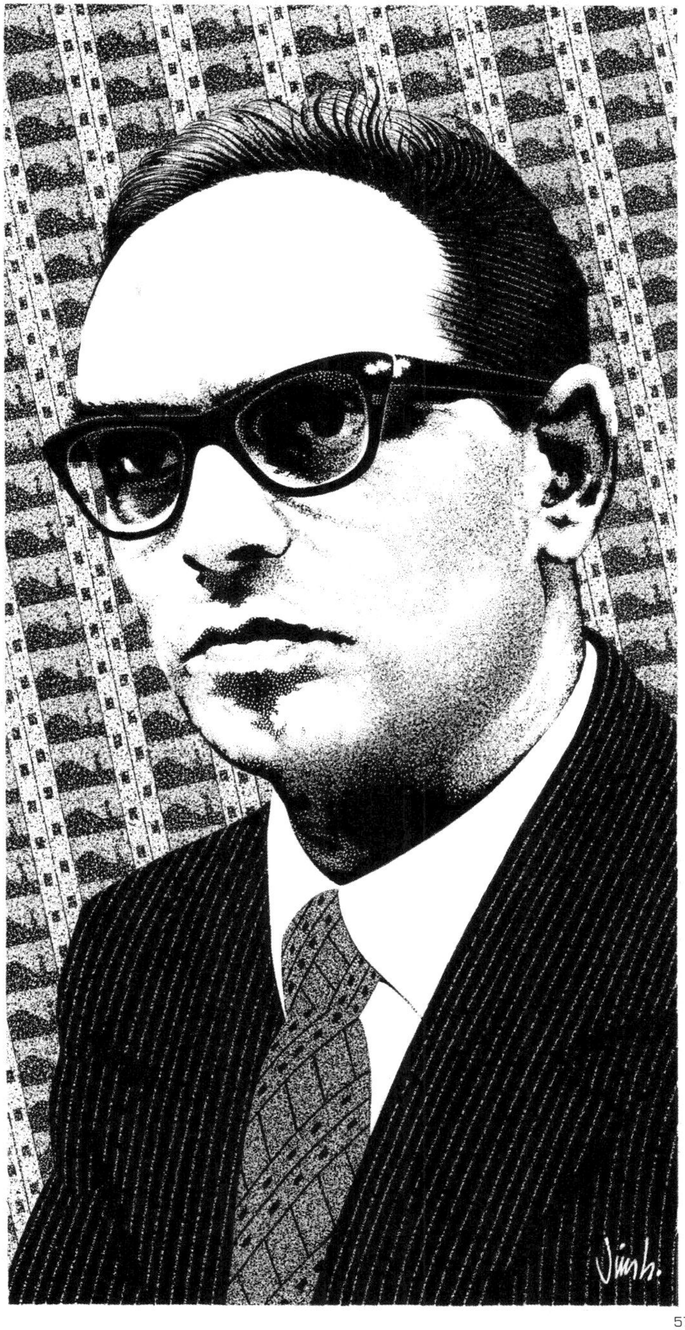

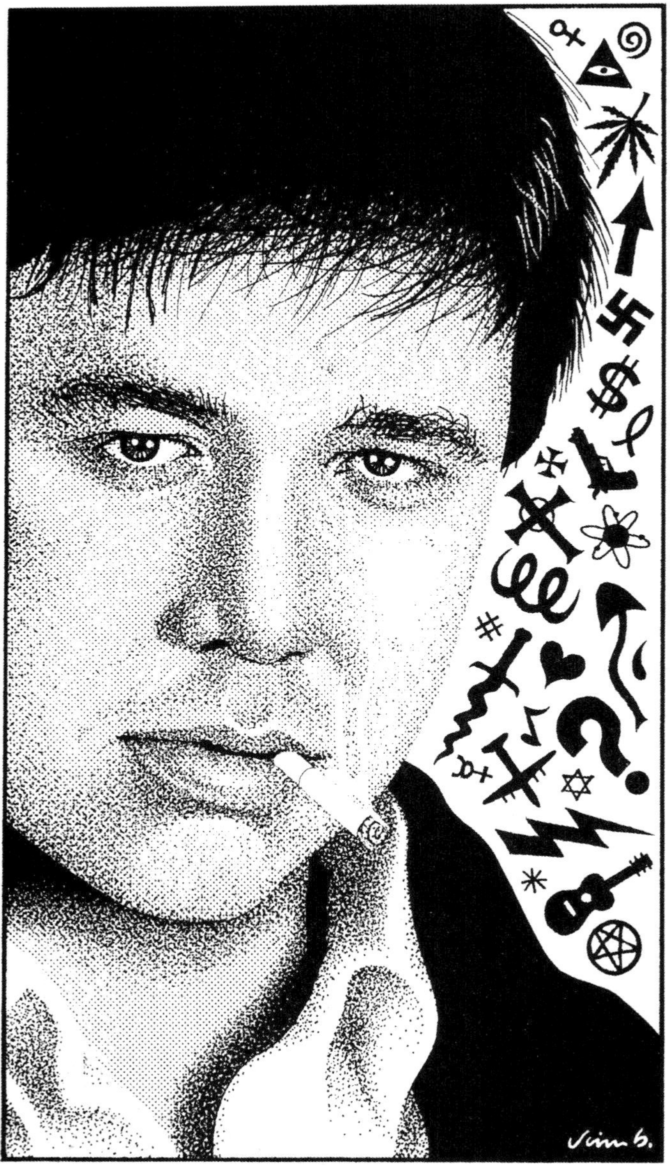

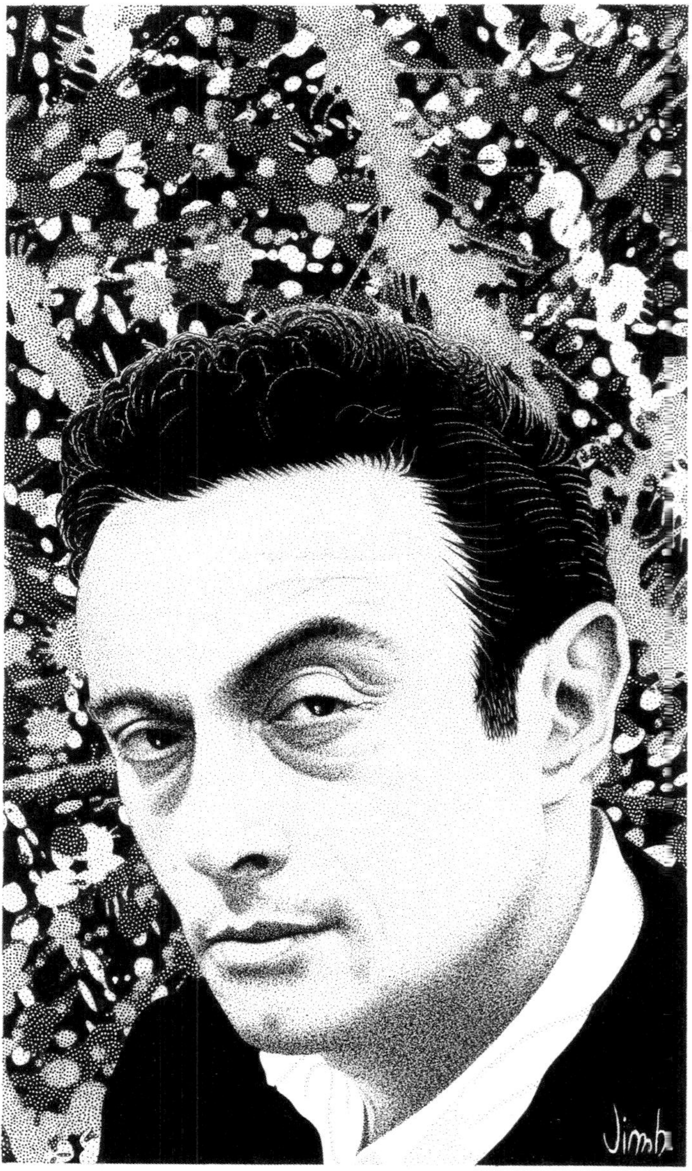

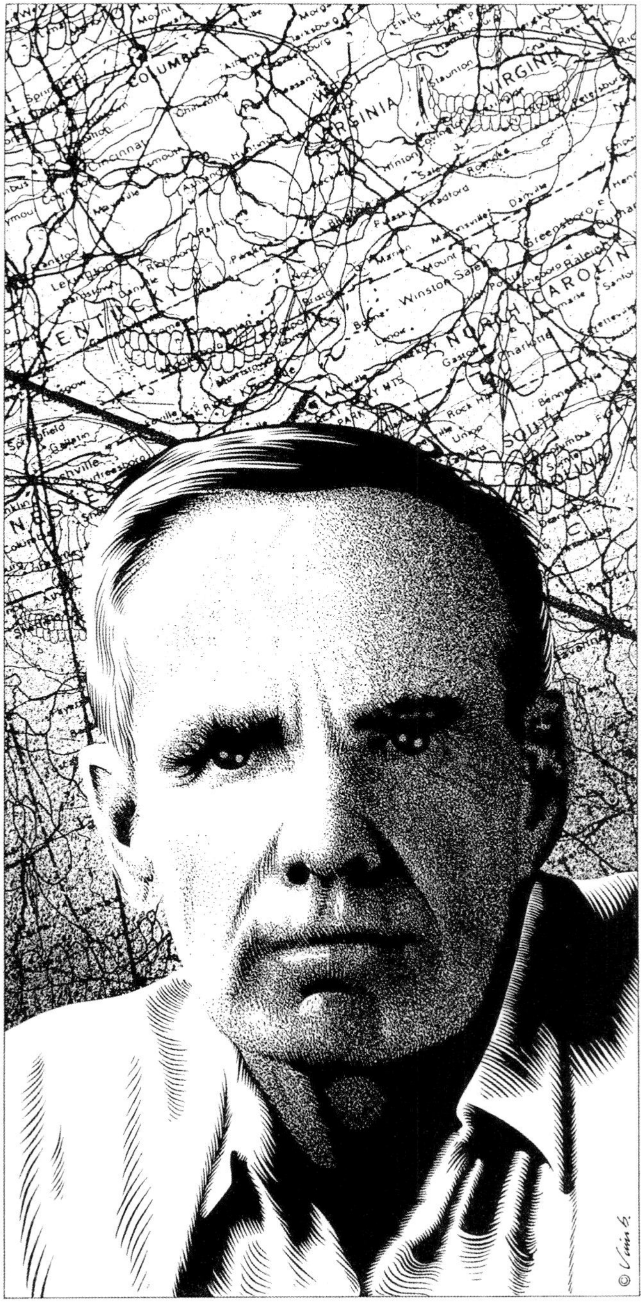

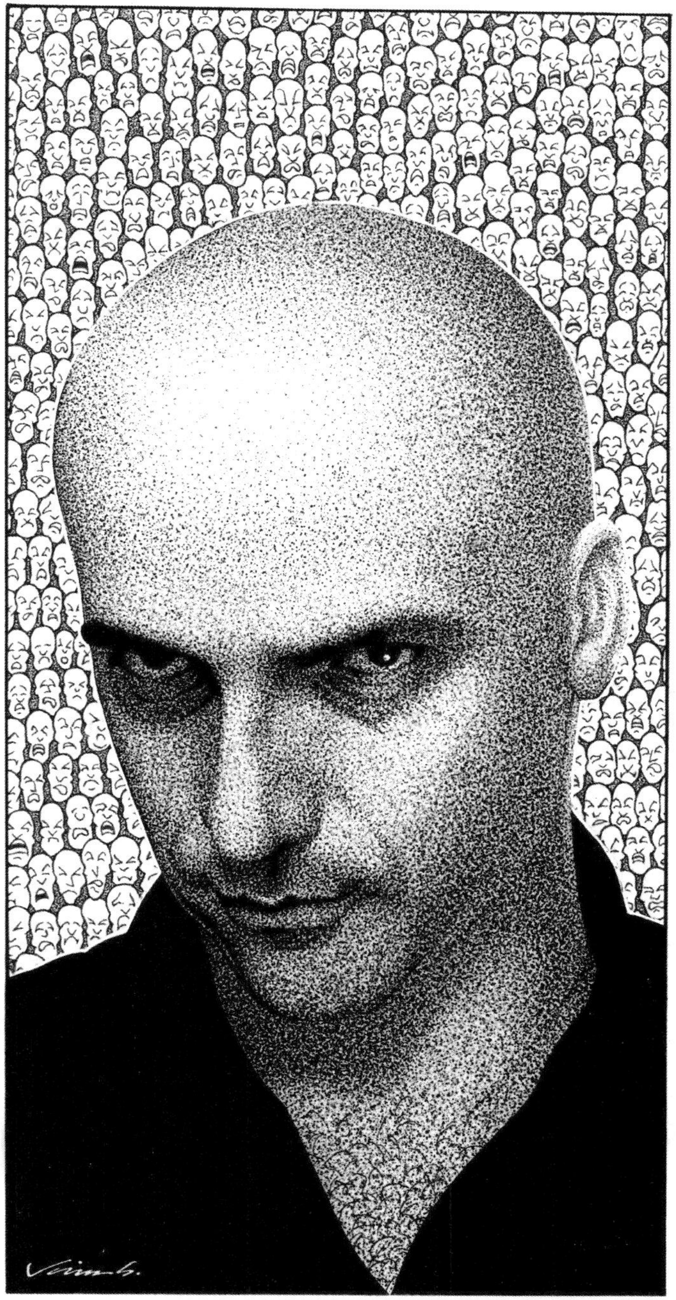

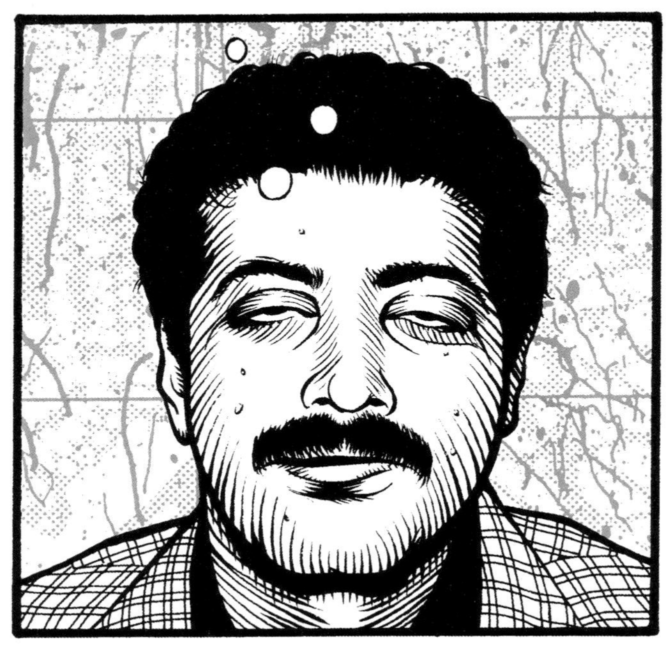

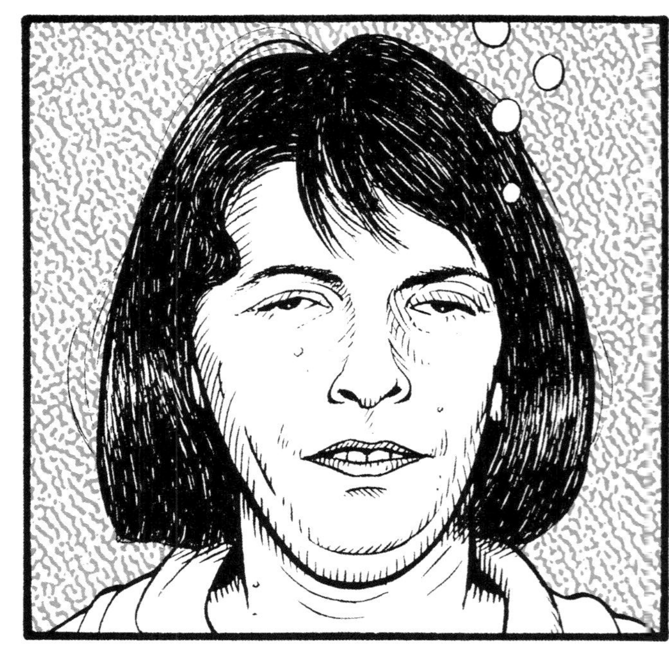

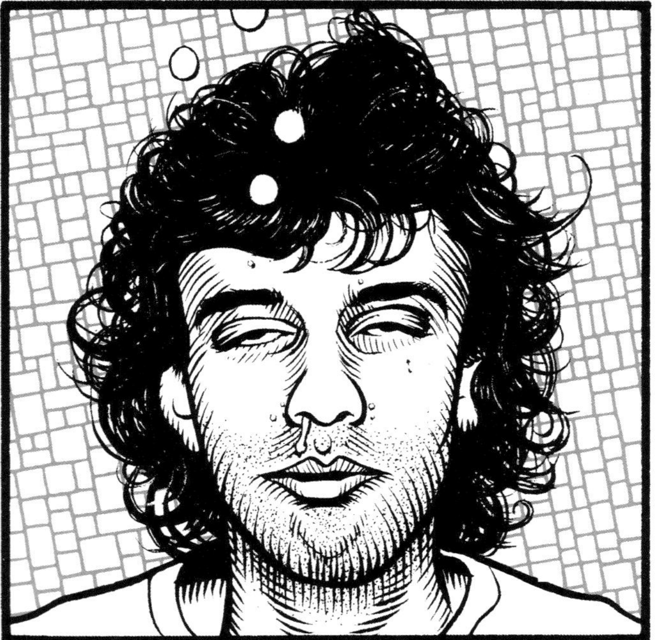

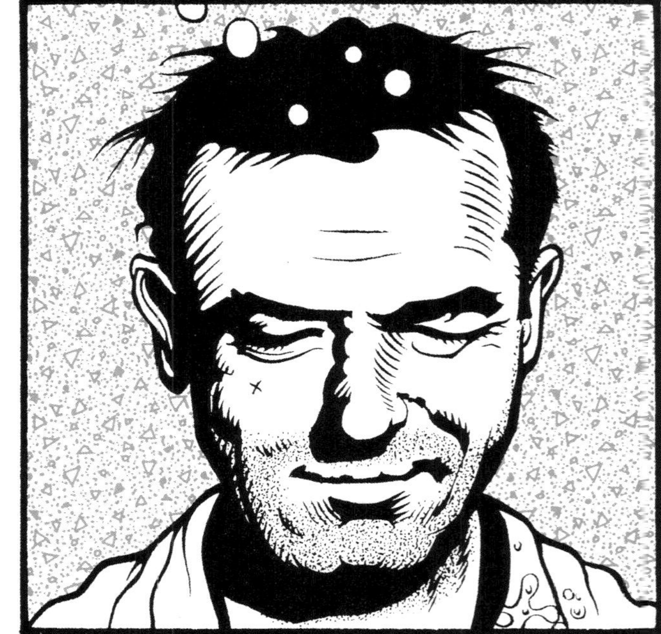

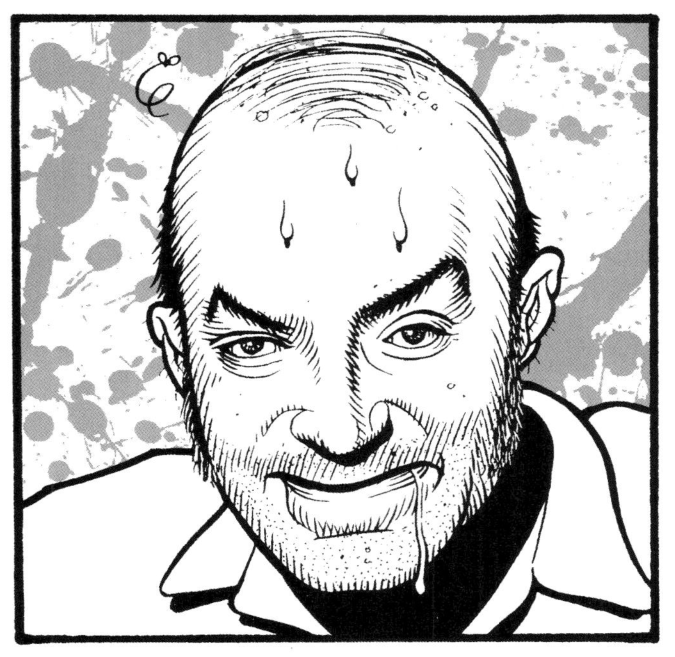

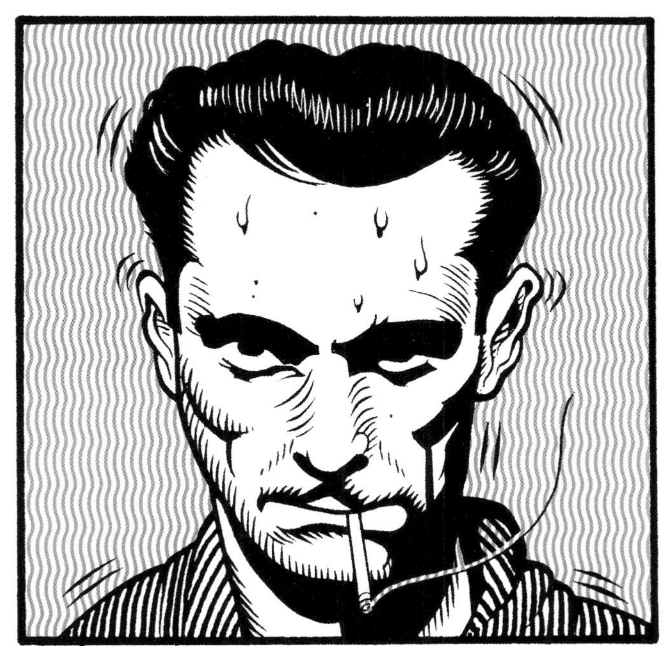

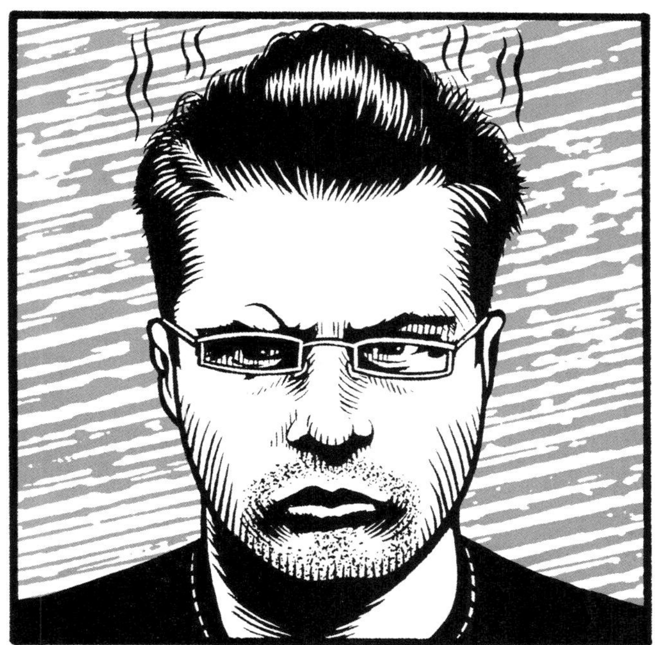

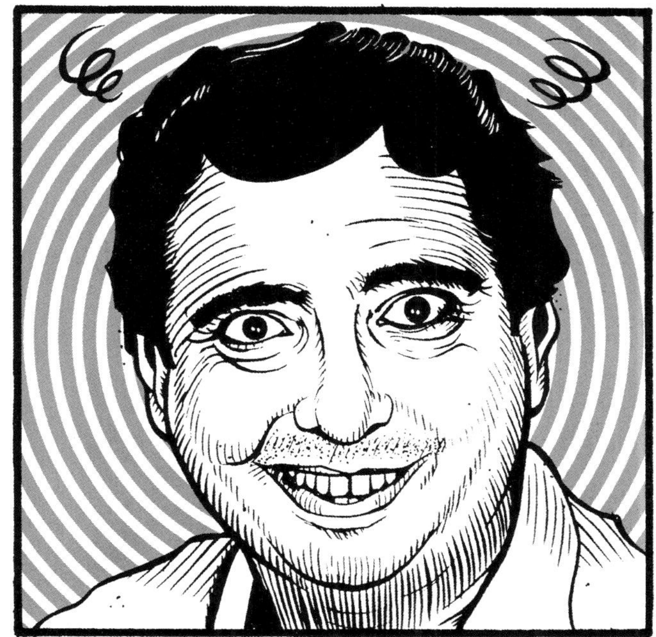

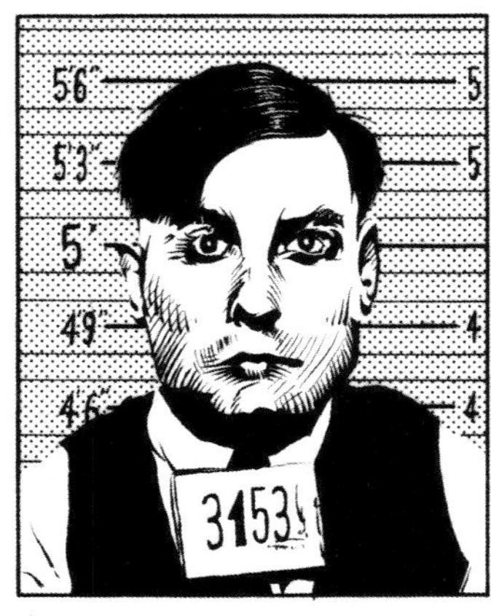
5'6"
5'3"
5'
4'9"
4'6"
3153

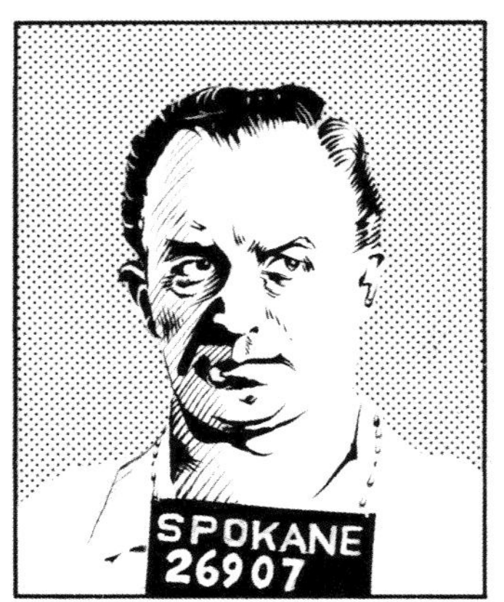
SPOKANE
26907

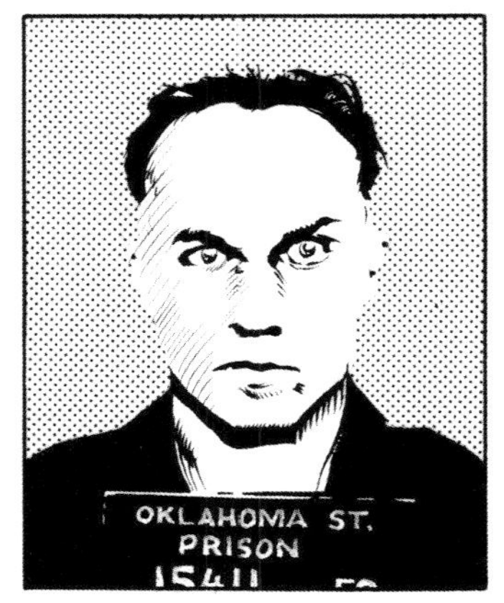
OKLAHOMA ST.
PRISON

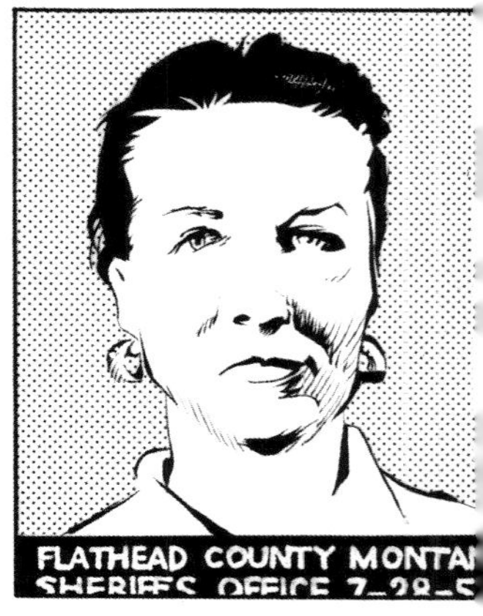
FLATHEAD COUNTY MONTA

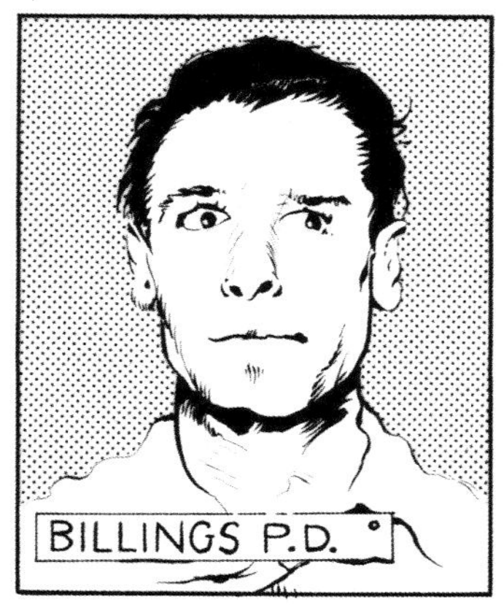
BILLINGS P.D.

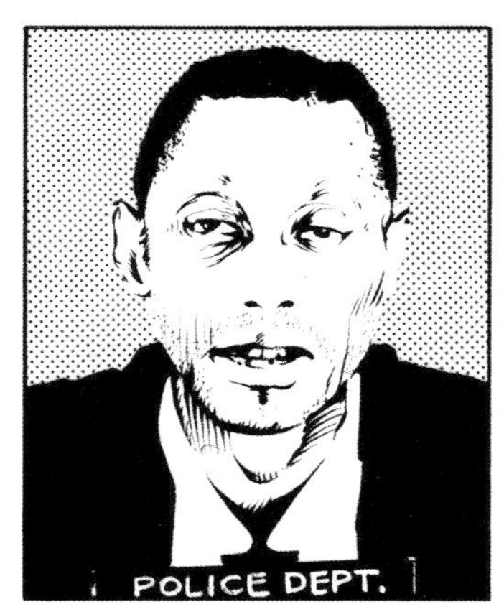
POLICE DEPT.

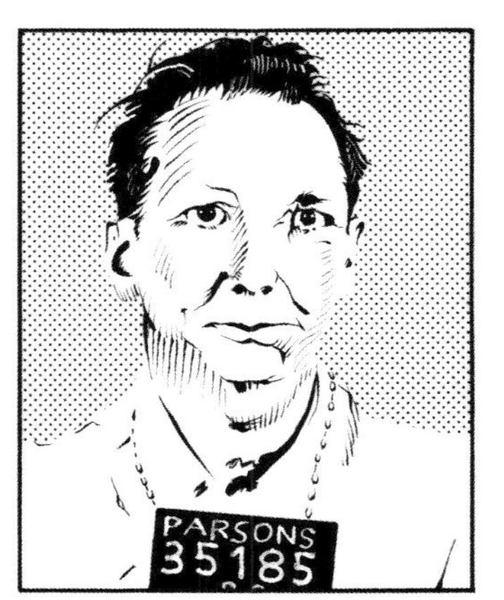
PARSONS
35185

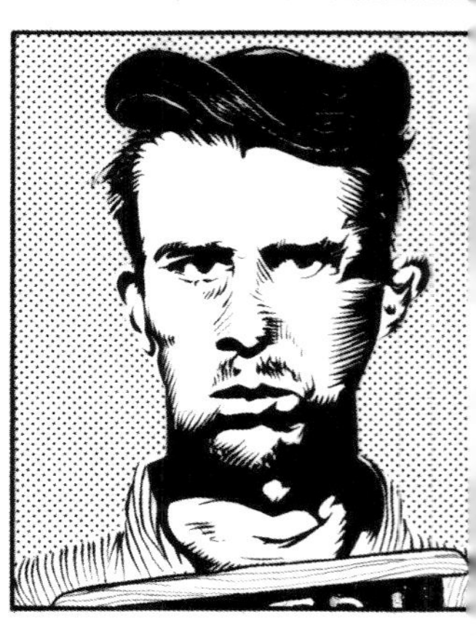

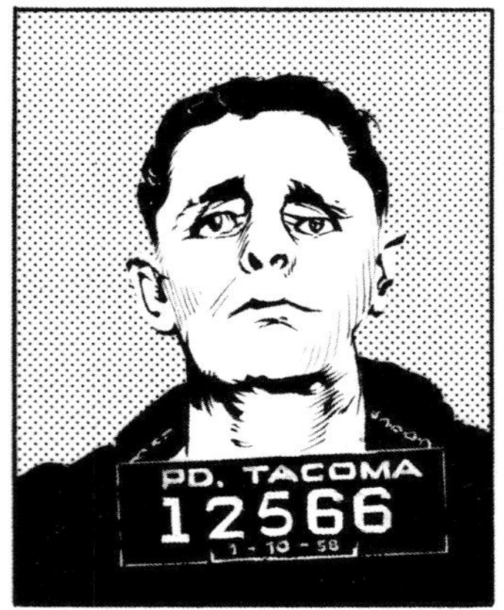
PD. TACOMA
12566
1-10-58

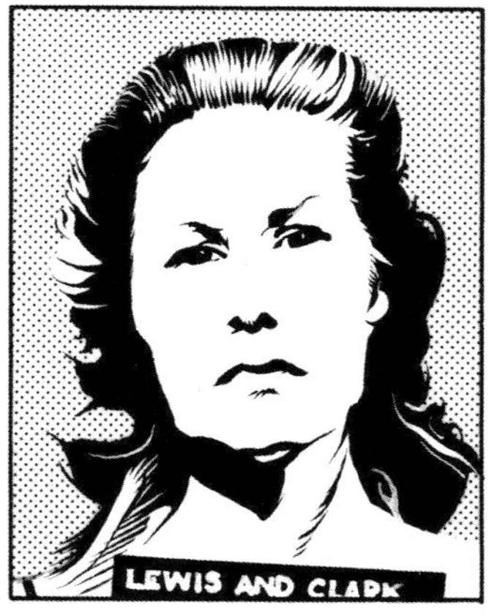
LEWIS AND CLARK

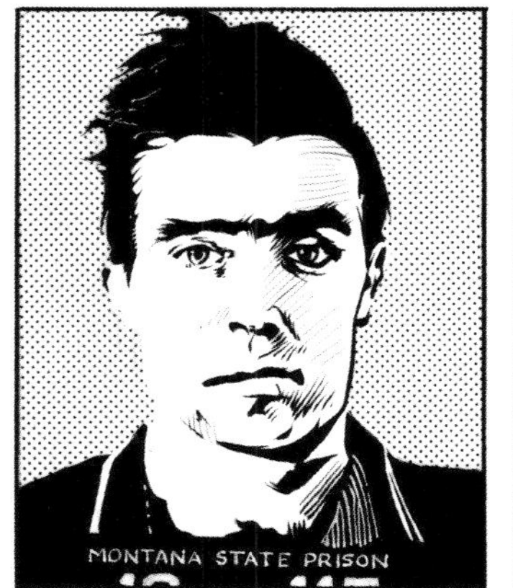
MONTANA STATE PRISON

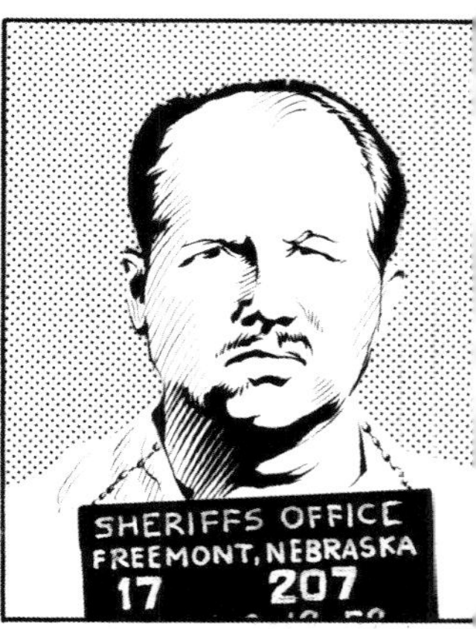
SHERIFFS OFFICE
FREEMONT, NEBRASKA
17 207

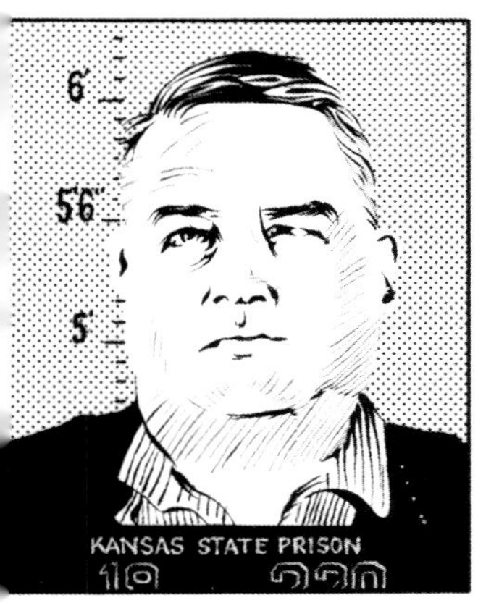
6'
5'6"
5'
KANSAS STATE PRISON

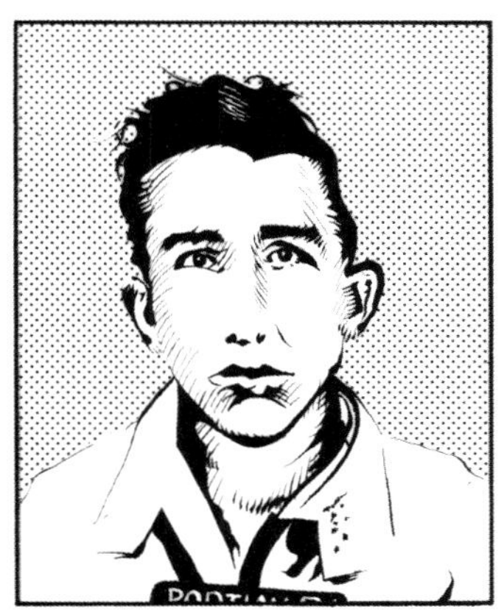

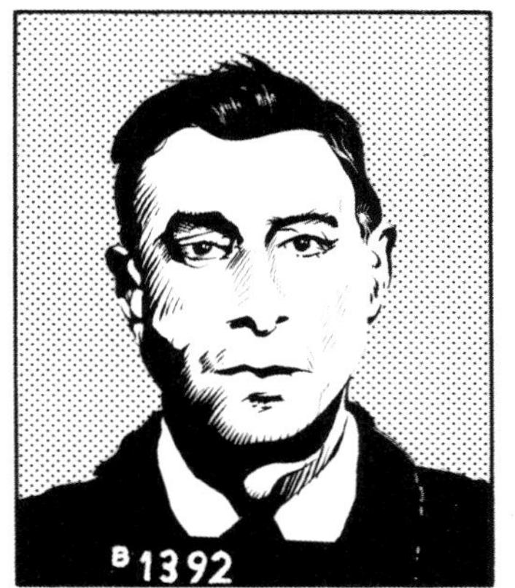
B1392

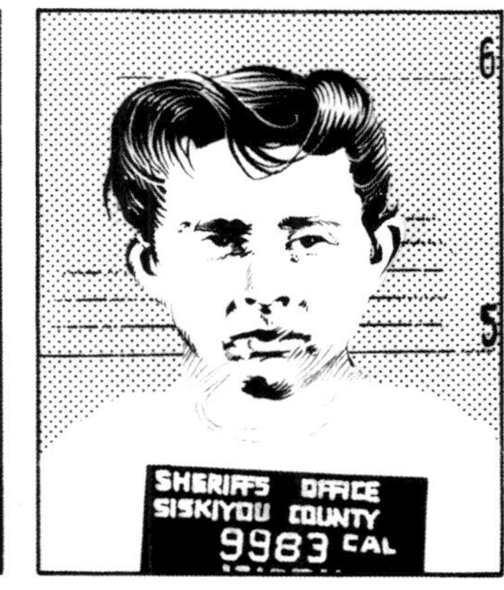
6
5
SHERIFFS OFFICE
SISKIYOU COUNTY
9983 CAL

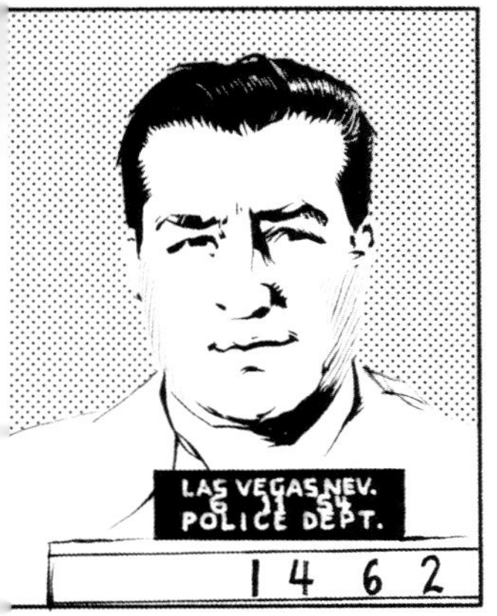
LAS VEGAS NEV.
6 11 54
POLICE DEPT.
1 4 6 2

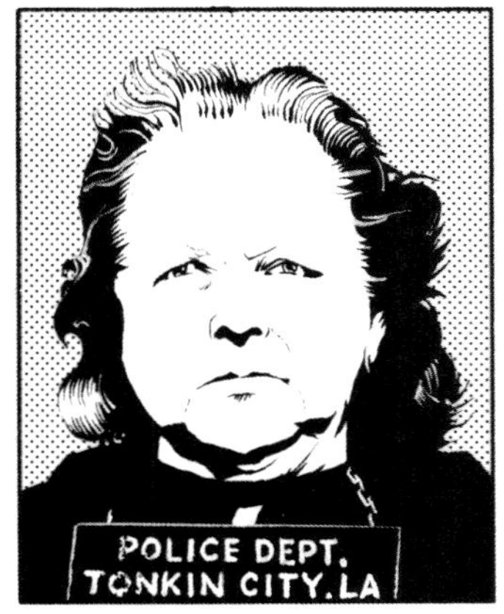
POLICE DEPT.
TONKIN CITY. LA

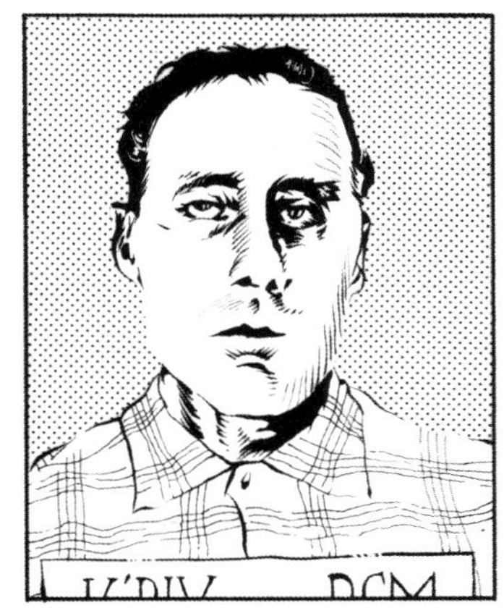

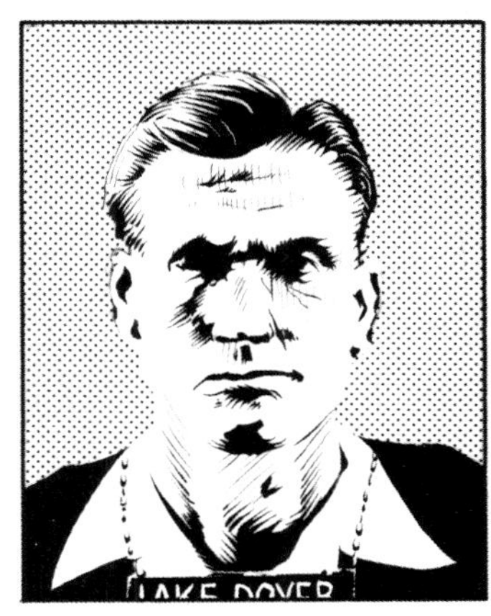

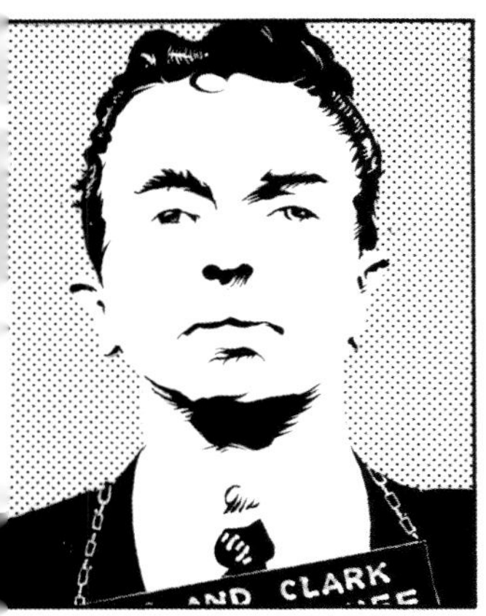
AND CLARK

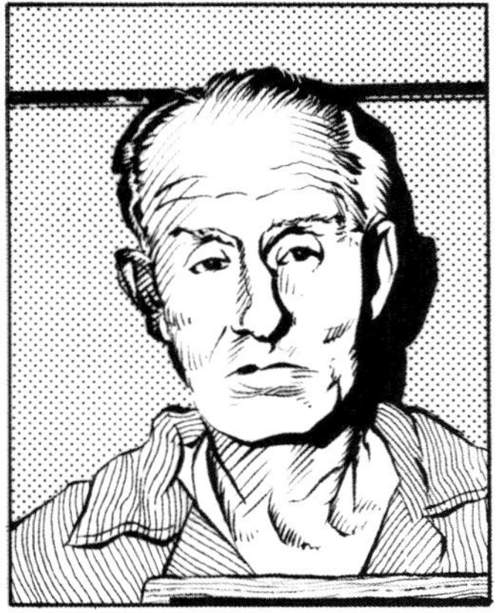

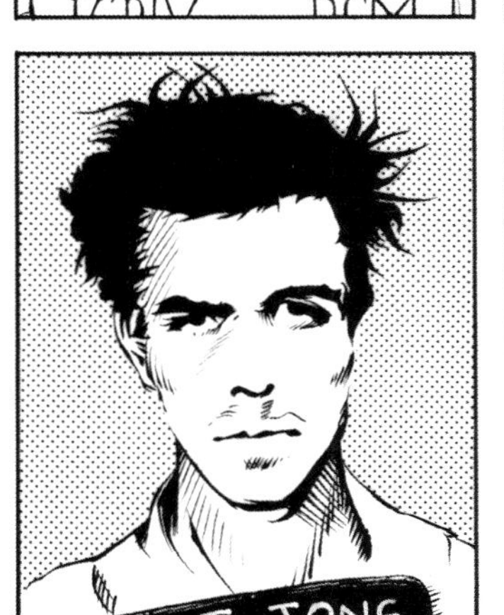

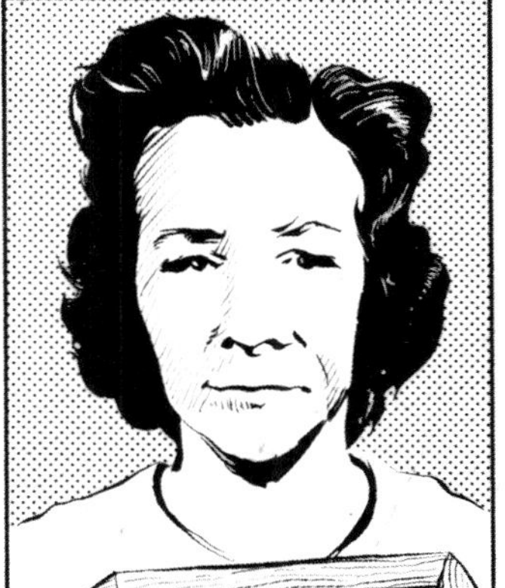

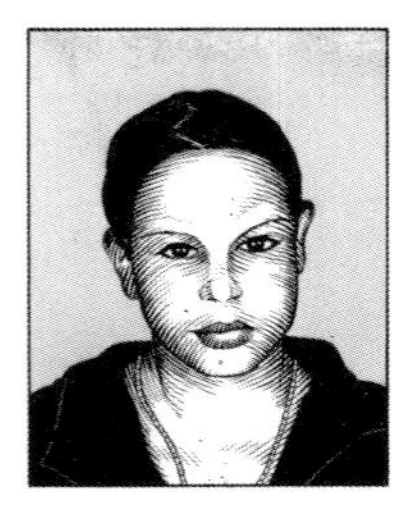
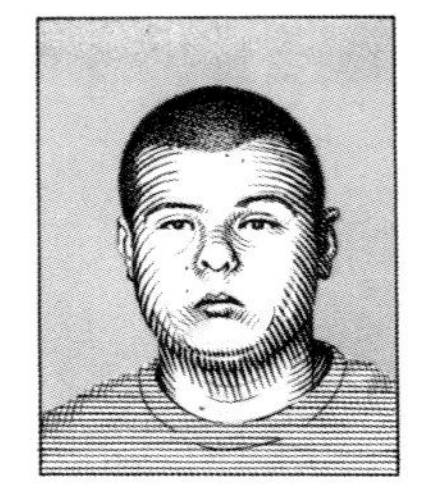
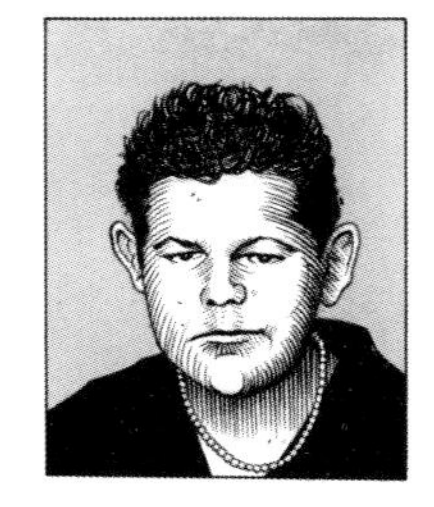
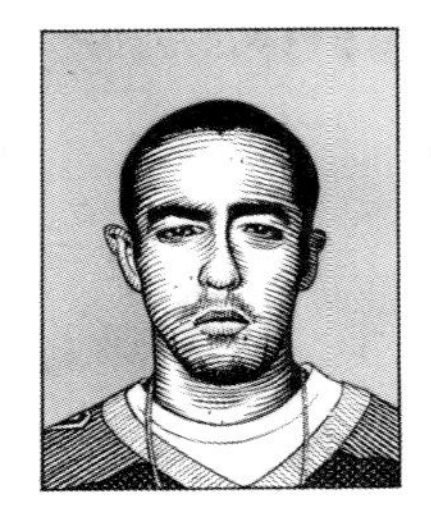
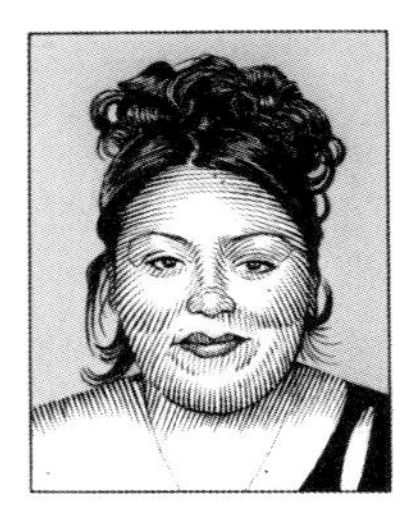
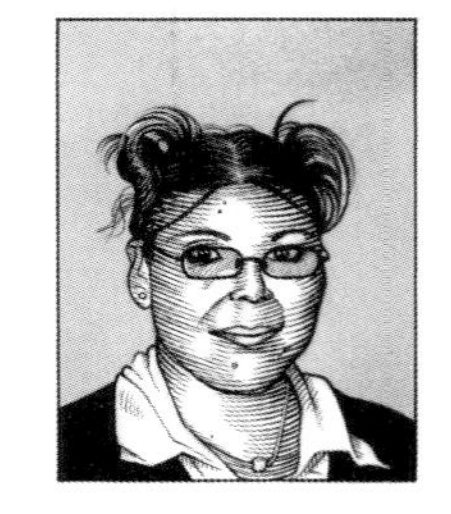
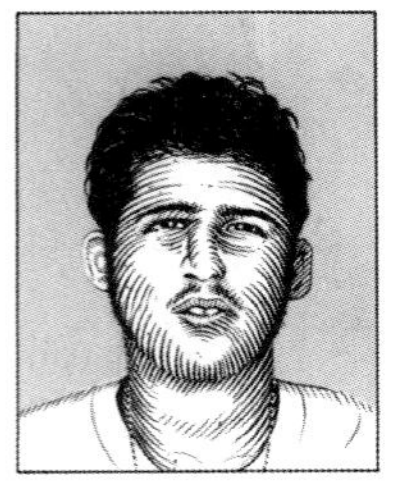
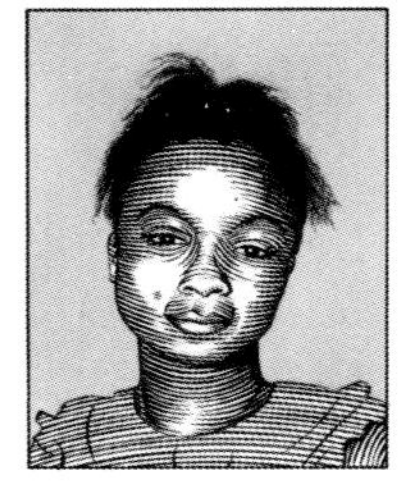
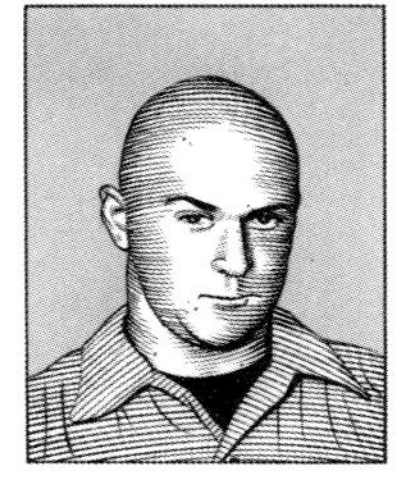
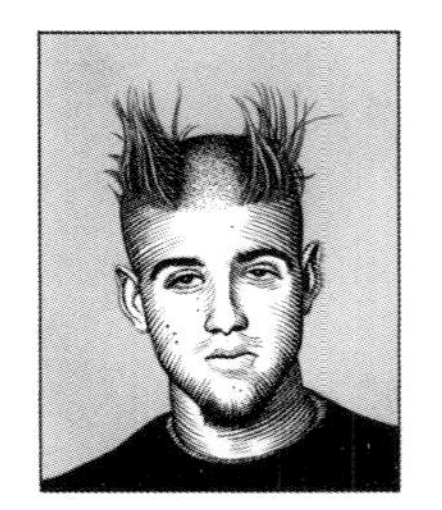
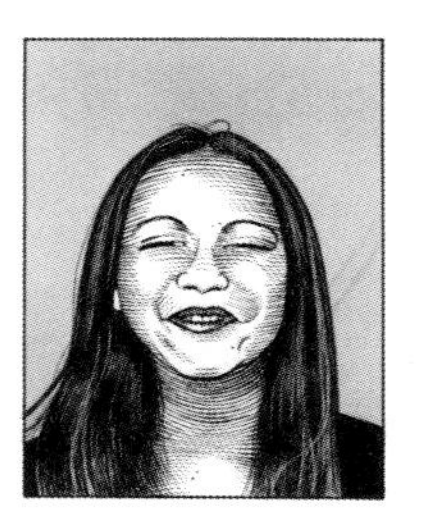
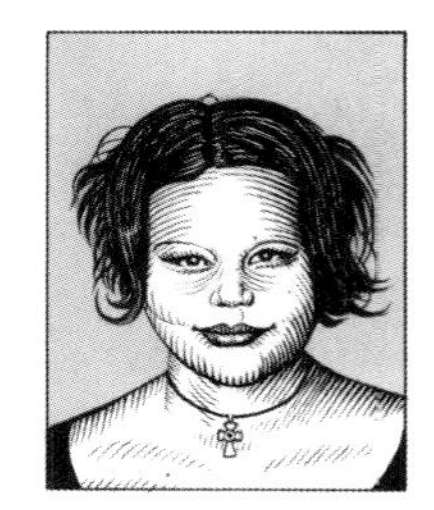
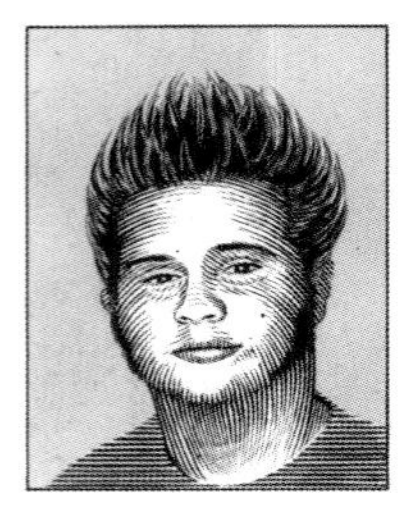
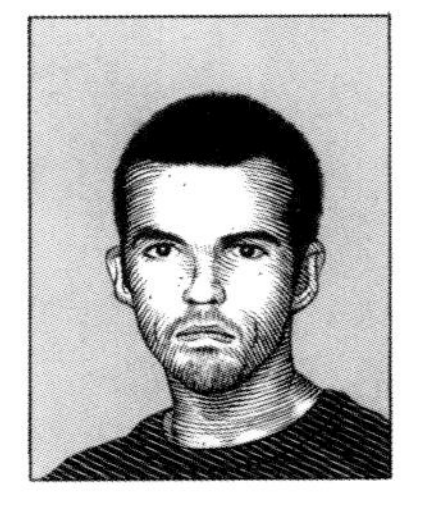
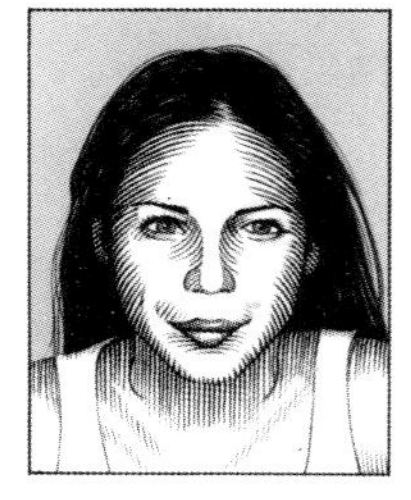
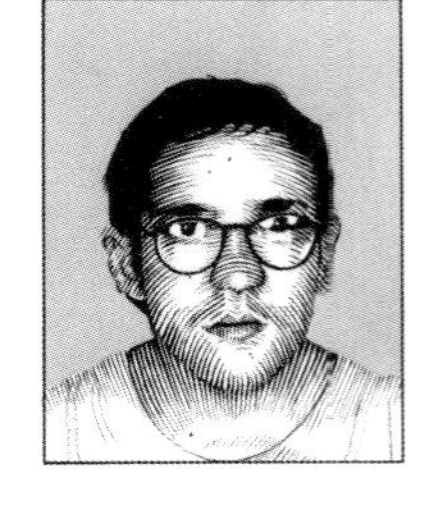
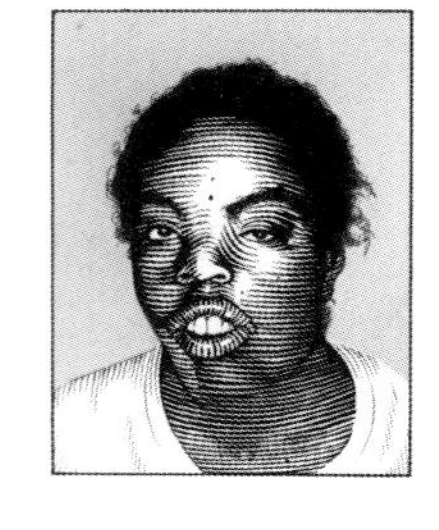
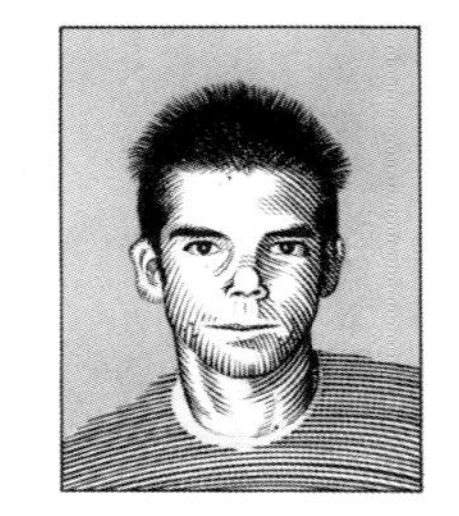
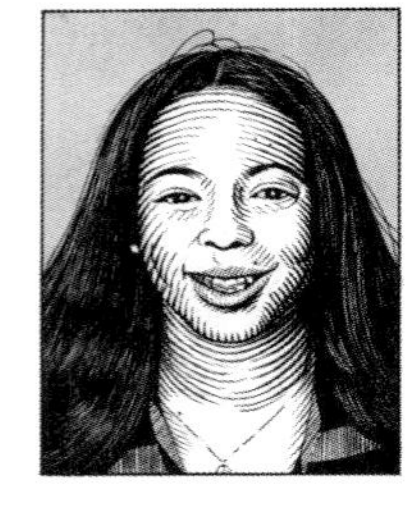
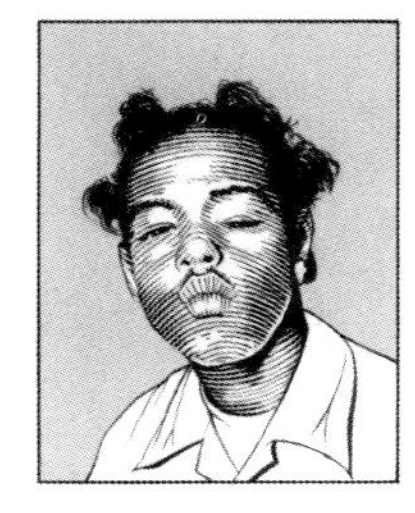
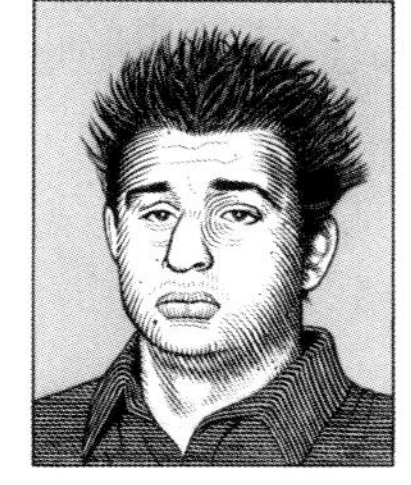
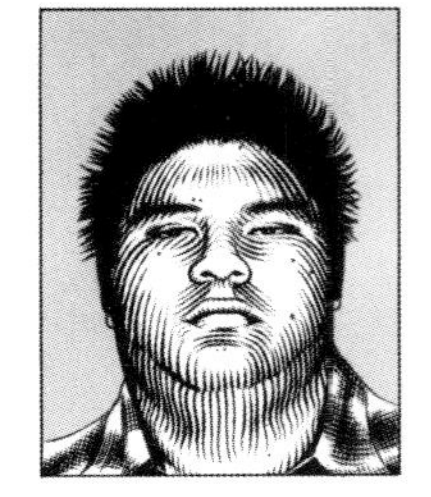
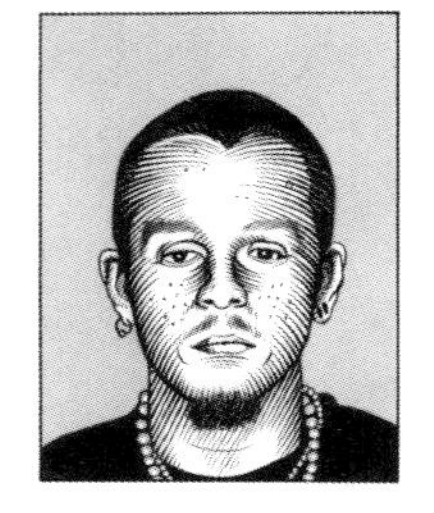
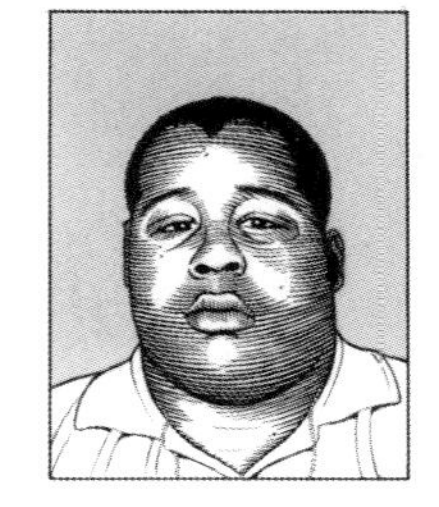
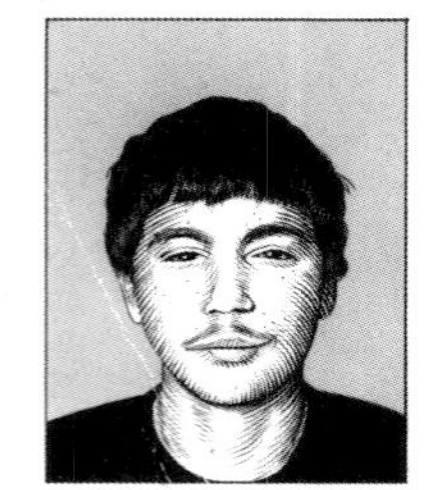
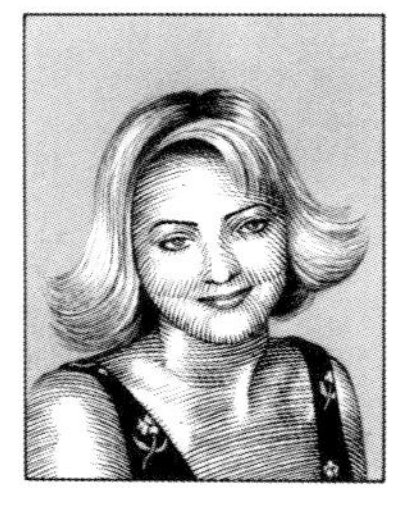
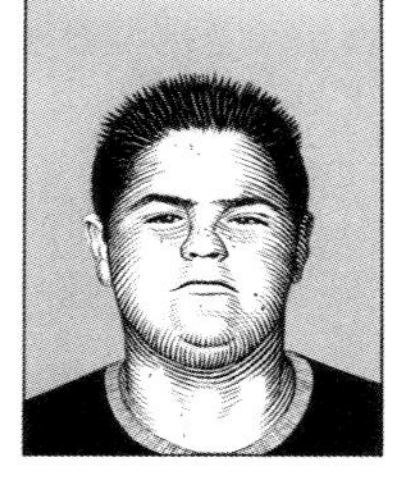
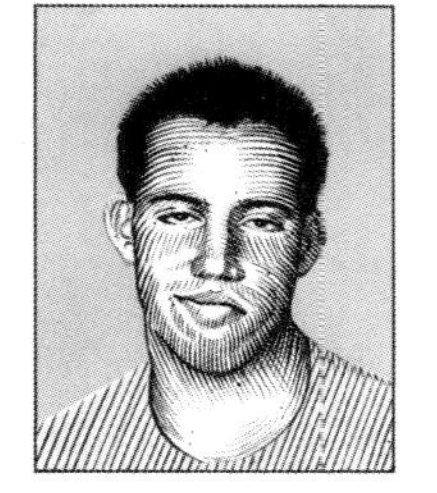
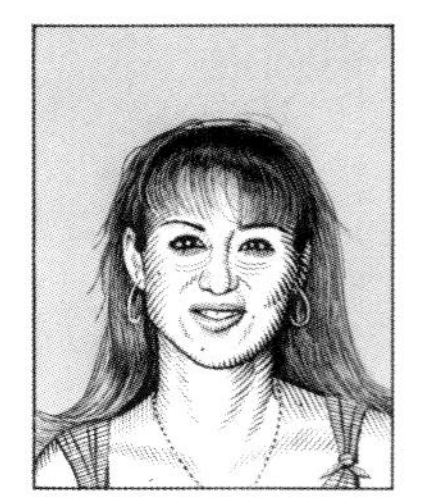
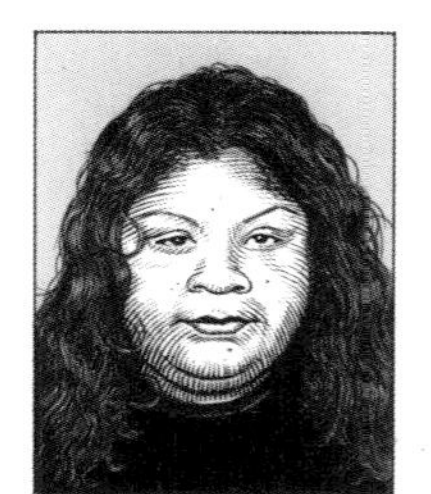